ESSENTIAL
DISNEYLAND® RESORT
PARIS

Original text by Lindsay Hunt

Updated by David Halford

© Automobile Association Developments Limited 2009
First published 2007
Reprinted 2009. Information verified and updated

ISBN: 978-0-7495-6008-9

Published by AA Publishing, a trading name of Automobile Association Developments
Limited, whose registered office is Fanum House, Basing View, Basingstoke,
Hampshire RG21 4EA. Registered number 1878835.

Essex County Council Libraries

About this book

This book is divided into six sections.

The essence of Disneyland® Resort Paris pages 6–19
Introduction; Features; Food and drink; Short break including the 10 Essentials

Planning pages 20–35
Before you go; Getting there; Getting around; Being there

The story so far pages 36–71
How Disneyland Resort Paris was created

Exploring pages 72–153
The unmissable highlights of a visit to Disneyland Resort Paris

Excursions pages 154–167
Places to visit nearby

Paris pages 168–187
The highlights of a visit to Paris

Admission prices
Inexpensive (under €7)
Moderate (€7–€11)
Expensive (over €11)

Hotel prices
Prices are per room per night in Paris and places to visit around Disneyland Resort Paris: € budget (under €100); €€ moderate (€100–€200); €€€ expensive to luxury (over €200)

Restaurant prices
Prices are for a three-course meal per person without drinks in Paris and places to visit around Disneyland Resort Paris: € budget (under €23); €€ moderate (€23–€80); €€€ expensive (over €80)

Contents

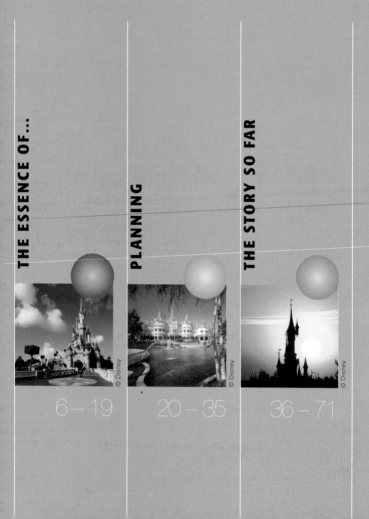

© Disney

© Disney

© Disney

EXPLORING...

EXCURSIONS

PARIS

© Disney

The essence of...

© Disney

© Dis.

The Disney® Parks imported from the US are now a central plank in France's tourism industry, attracting millions of visitors annually from all over Europe. Here fantasy, humour, excitement and the latest technology ensure a memorable visit.

Besides Disneyland® Park and Walt Disney Studios® Park, a medley of eye-catching, American-styled hotels may tempt you to extend your stay.

features

DISNEYLAND® RESORT PARIS IN FIGURES

● Disneyland Resort Paris extends over a site measuring 1,943ha (4,801 acres) – one-fifth the size of Paris

● Approximately 900ha (2,224 acres) have so far been developed

● Around 175 million visitors have been to the resort since it first opened in 1992

● Annual attendance figures exceed 14 million (14.5 million in 2007)

● 40 per cent of the resort's visitors hail from France, and about 19 per cent from the UK

● On average in any year, more than 12,500 employees (Cast Members) from 100 different nationalities work at Disneyland Resort Paris, including over 700 artists – actors, dancers, musicians, designers, couturiers, etc

● Disney® Village is one of the largest entertainment complexes in the Île de France, featuring over 30,000sq m (323,000sq ft) of themed dining, shopping and leisure activities

● The resort now incorporates 60 different attractions

© Disney

© Disney

© Disney

© Disney

- 840 parades are staged each year in the Disneyland® Park
- Sleeping Beauty Castle is 43m (141ft) high
- The buildings on Main Street, U.S.A.® contain 580,000 bricks and are lit by 225,000 separate light bulbs, re-creating the atmosphere of New York at the turn of the 20th century
- The catapult launch system at Space Mountain: Mission 2 induces a G-force measuring 1.3 Newtons
- Catastrophe Canyon® in Walt Disney Studios® Park uses 265,000 litres (58,300 gallons) of water for each display – the water is recycled for each show
- The 68 or so food and beverage outlets dish up around 30 million meals per year

© Disney

food & drink

Eating Disney-style is all part of the Disney® Park experience. Choice is extensive, but the only food shops and restaurants within reasonable walking distance of the resort are operated by Disney. Picnic tables are provided near the Disneyland® Hotel for guests who bring their own supplies, but remember, you are not allowed to take any food or drinks into either of the Disney Parks. Unlike the US Disney Parks, alcohol is served in the restaurants.

EATING DISNEY STYLE

Nearly 70 eateries serve a range of international dishes within the Disney resort. Some have table or buffet service (what Disney refers to as 'fine dining'), while at others you queue by counters for fast food like pizzas and burgers ('food to go'). Some are no more than take-away snack bars. Scattered around both parks, seasonal *chariots gourmands* (food carts and kiosks) deal with any sudden hunger pangs by dispensing bagels, muffins, stir-fries, popcorn, ice-cream and soft drinks. Most of the Disney Park restaurants stay open all day, but at quiet times of year you may find some of them closed, sometimes in rotation.

© Disney

© Disney

© Disney

Outside the Disney Parks, the Disney® Hotels each contain attractively themed restaurants. All of these are open to non-residents, but it is always advisable to reserve a table in advance. Disney® Village offers a further dozen or so eating places, including a book-ahead dinner-show venue. All Disney restaurants serve vegetarian dishes, and special diets (kosher, for instance) or food intolerances can be catered for if you give notice of your requirements. Advance bookings can be made at any Disney table-service or buffet restaurant on a central reservation number: 01 60 30 40 50.

Naturally enough in the Disney universe, special efforts are made for younger guests. Child menus or child-sized portions are available at table- or

© Disney

© Disney

counter-service restaurants, along with baby food and high chairs on request. Disney characters visit certain restaurants to introduce themselves over a meal, such as at Café Mickey or the Lucky Nugget Saloon (generally for an additional charge). Look out for free child menu offers during quiet periods (eg 3–5pm in Disney® Village).

FAST FOOD

At peak times the restaurants within the resort dish up around 150,000 meals a day. Considering the speed at which such industrial quantities of fast food are handled, the quality is surprisingly good. There is some awareness of prevailing trends towards healthier, less fat-laden diets, and of the preferences of vegetarian guests. Ambience makes all the difference. Where else in France could you dine on a palm-fringed Caribbean shore with boats gliding past your table, or munch spare ribs in a high-raftered Wild West barn full of wagon wheels and hay rakes?

short break

However long you have to visit Disneyland® Resort Paris, try some of the following to capture the real flavour of the Disney® Parks. These suggestions will give you a wide range of experiences, and will make your visit memorable.

DISNEYLAND® PARK

● **Watch the Disney night-time parade** (seasonal) with its twinkling lights and favourite Disney characters.

● **Ride Space Mountain: Mission 2** in Discoveryland for the ultimate in galactic travel. Blast off from the rocket ship for a trip into space.

● **Big Thunder Mountain** in Frontierland is a must for thrill seekers as you hurtle through the rocky landscape and deep into a mine.

● **Experience a high-speed thrill** on Indiana Jones™ and the Temple of Peril, an adrenalin-fuelled roller coaster in Adventureland. This ride ends in a dramatic loop-the-loop.

● **Pirates of the Caribbean,** located in Adventureland, is one of the most realistic attractions in the Disneyland Park. It has great special effects, full of swashbuckling adventure.

● **Sleeping Beauty Castle** in Fantasyland is every child's interpretation of fairyland and a main landmark of the Disneyland Park.

● **Undergo a 3-D 'shrinking' experience** by watching Honey, I Shrunk the Audience in Discoveryland. A host of special effects are employed for a really original sensation.

- **Take in a show** from the schedule of spectacular performances that include The Legend of the Lion King and High School Musical (seasonal).

- **Thwart the Evil Emperor's plans** and save the toy universe at the Buzz Lightyear Laser Blast.

WALT DISNEY STUDIOS® PARK

- **Studio Tram Tour®: Behind the Magic** featuring Catastrophe Canyon® is not just a tour round the studio; stand by for an exciting trip.

- **Check out Moteurs…Action! Stunt Show Spectacular®** in Backlot at Walt Disney Studios Park for the best in thrilling cinema stunts featuring cars and motorcycles on a realistic film set.

Planning

© Disney

Before you go

WHEN TO GO

JAN	FEB	MAR	APR	MAY	JUN	JUL	AUG	SEP	OCT	NOV	DEC
7°C	7°C	10°C	16°C	17°C	23°C	25°C	26°C	21°C	16°C	12°C	8°C
45°F	45°F	50°F	61°F	63°F	73°F	77°F	79°F	70°F	61°F	54°F	46°F

High season   Low season

Marne-la-Vallée's climate is rather drier than that of coastal France. The wettest months are from November to January and from March to May (all have more than 15 days of rainfall – not necessarily, of course, all day long).

Highest temperatures are predictably in July and August, when a sunhat is advisable. Between May and June and September and October there are pleasantly equable temperatures, and daytime highs are between 16°C and 21°C (61°C and 70°F). Otherwise, it is unusual to experience climatic extremes or sharp seasonal variations. Average temperatures stay above freezing all year round, and it rarely gets too hot to stay outside in the middle of the day.

WHAT YOU NEED

		UK	Germany	USA	Canada	Australia	Ireland	Netherlands	Spain
● Required	Some countries require a passport to remain valid for a minimum period (usually at least six months) beyond the date of entry – check before you travel.								
○ Suggested									
▲ Not required									
Passport (or National Identity Card where applicable)		●	●	●	●	●	●	●	●
Visa (regulations can change – check before you travel)		▲	▲	▲	▲	▲	▲	▲	▲
Onward or Return Ticket		▲	▲	▲	▲	▲	▲	▲	▲
Health Inoculations (tetanus and polio)		▲	▲	▲	▲	▲	▲	▲	▲
Health Documentation (► 23, Health insurance)		●	●	●	●	●	●	●	●
Travel Insurance		○	○	○	○	○	○	○	○
Driving Licence (national)		●	●	●	●	●	●	●	●
Car Insurance Certificate		○	○	n/a	n/a	n/a	○	○	○
Car Registration Document		●	●	n/a	n/a	n/a	●	●	●

TOURIST OFFICES AT HOME
In the UK
Maison de la France
Lincoln House, 300 High Holborn,
London WC1V 7JH
☎ 09068 244123
www.franceguide.com

In the USA
Maison de la France
825 Third Avenue, 29th floor

(entrance on 50th Street),
New York NY10022
☎ 514/288 1904

Maison de la France
9454 Wilshire Boulevard,
Suite 210, Beverly Hills CA90212
☎ 310/271 6665

HEALTH INSURANCE
Nationals of EU countries can obtain medical treatment at reduced cost in France with a European Health Insurance Card (EHIC), available from the Post Office, although private medical insurance is still advised and is essential for all other visitors.

Minor ailments can often be treated at pharmacies. All public hospitals have a 24-hour emergency service *(urgences)* as well as specialist doctors. Payment is made on the spot, but if you are hospitalized ask to see the *assistante sociale* to arrange payment directly through your medical insurance.

As for general medical treatment, nationals of EU countries can obtain dental treatment at reduced cost. Around 70 per cent of standard dentists' fees are refunded, but private medical insurance is advised for all.

TIME DIFFERENCES

GMT	France	Spain	USA (NY)	USA (West Coast)	Sydney
12 noon	1PM	1PM	7AM	4AM	10PM

France is on Central European Time (GMT+1). From late March, when clocks are put forward one hour, until late October, French summer time (GMT+2) operates.

DATES TO AVOID

You may be tied to school holiday times, but if you don't like crowds, try to avoid visiting during the popular French national holidays (► 26). You can also expect more crowds around Easter and Whitsuntide.

French school holidays are staggered, lasting several weeks (mid-April to mid-May; early July to early September). August is a traditional holiday month for many Parisians who may well visit Disneyland® Resort Paris then.

RESERVATIONS AND ADVANCE PLANNING

To reserve accommodation or to rent cars at Disneyland Resort Paris, call Reservations on 08705 03 03 03 (national rate call), seven days a week. From Eire, dial 00331 60 30 60 53 (international rate call) from Monday to Friday 8am– 8pm, Saturday 9am– 6pm (5pm on Sunday). You can also visit the Disneyland Resort Paris website: www.disneylandparis.co.uk or www.disneylandparis.com for more information. Inside France, tel: 01 60 30 60 53.

TIGHT BUDGET

Taking a family to Disneyland Resort Paris is by no means a budget option but there are ways to cut the costs.

© Disney

● All those ice-creams, soft drinks, T-shirts and mouse ears soon mount up to a hefty bill. Resist too many impulse buys.

● Choose counter-service cafés or food cart snacks rather than the more expensive table-service restaurants. Or bring a picnic to the picnic area between guest parking and the Disney® Parks.

● Families and friends can save money by sharing a room – all the Disney® Hotels have rooms suitable for parties of four (Disney's Davy Crockett Ranch® 2-bedroom log cabins sleep six).

● You can stay at one of the many non-Disney hotels scattered around the resort, or even in central Paris. Choose somewhere convenient for public transport if you don't have the use of a vehicle.

● Buying two separate 1-day Park tickets and spending a day in each Park might save a few euros on the current cost of a 2-Day Hopper, but the best-value option for most visitors is a 3-Day Hopper, allowing free movement between both Parks within the allotted time frame. You don't have to use your ticket on consecutive days; tickets remain valid for 1 year from the date on the back of the ticket.

● Take some light rainwear to avoid buying Mickey Mouse ponchos or umbrellas if it rains.

● Try to avoid the expensive video games arcades.

NATIONAL HOLIDAYS

1 Jan *New Year's Day*
Mar/Apr *Easter Sunday and Monday*
1 May *Labour Day*
May *Ascension Day*
May/Jun *Whit Sunday and Monday*

14 Jul *Bastille Day*
15 Aug *Assumption Day*
1 Nov *All Saints' Day*
11 Nov *Remembrance Day*
25 Dec *Christmas Day*

Banks, businesses, museums and most shops (except boulangeries) are closed on these days, but this does not apply to Disneyland® Resort Paris.

WHAT'S ON WHEN

DISNEYLAND® RESORT PARIS

Besides the big parades that take place daily, or whenever Disneyland® Park is open late, special holidays are marked by extra-spectacular extravaganzas. New Year witnesses even more fireworks than usual and parties in all the hotels. Special parades are held periodically throughout the year. Needless to say, Christmas is celebrated with carols and a tree. Other events are planned at shorter notice during the year.

PARIS

January/February *La Grande Parade de Paris:* The Parisian New Year festival takes place in different venues around the city (www.parisparade.com).
Chinese New Year: Dragon parades and other festivities in Chinatown.

March/April *Marathon International de Paris:* Starting from place de la Concorde and finishing on avenue Foch behind the Arc de Triomphe.

April/May *International Paris Fair:* Food, homes and gardens and much more at Porte de Versailles.

May–June *Labour Day* (1 May): Processions.
Paris Jazz Festival: Free concerts on summer weekend afternoons.
Festival Foire Saint-Germain (Jun): Village traditions revived.
Fête de la Musique (21 Jun): Everything from classical to techno, both indoors and out.

July–August *Bastille Day* (14 Jul): This highly significant date is celebrated with fireworks and street dances on the evening of the 13th and a parade on the 14th on the Champs-Élysées.

Paris, Quartier d'Eté: Open-air music, plays and dance.

Fête des Tuileries: Jardin des Tuileries becomes a fairground (begins end of June).

September *Festival d'Automne* (mid Sep–end Dec): Music, theatre and dance throughout the city.

October *Foire Internationale d'Art Contemporain:* Paris's biggest modern art fair, at the Grand Palais and Cour Carré du Louvre.

December *Salon Nautique International:* International boat show at Paris Expo, Porte de Versailles.

© Disney

OTHER OPTIONS

Many places within easy reach of Disneyland® Resort Paris hold special events.

Meaux has a summer festival with *son et lumière* shows in the grounds of the Bishop's Palace.

Reims celebrates when champagne grapes are harvested.

Versailles puts on grand fountain shows in summer.

At **Fontainebleau** the atmosphere of belle époque Paris is re-enacted with costumed actors strolling through the gardens.

Vaux-le-Vicomte offers candlelight tours on certain evenings. Details of all events are available at the tourist office near Marne-la-Vallée station.

Getting there

BY AIR

Orly Airport

N/A

55 minutes

60km (37 miles) to Disneyland® Resort   55 minutes

Roissy-Charles de Gaulle Airport

20 minutes

35 minutes

40km (25 miles) to Disneyland® Resort   35 minutes

Paris has two main airports (www.aeroportsdeparis.fr), Roissy-Charles de Gaulle (tel: 01 48 62 22 80), where most international flights arrive, and Orly (tel: 01 49 75 15 15). Both are served by shuttle buses (*navettes*) which depart for Disneyland® Resort Paris every 30 minutes at peak times, every hour at other times. Journey times vary according to traffic density. Buses cost the same from either airport (adult €16, child 3–11 years €13; transfer fares are included in Disney® Hotel packages). Passengers are taken to each of the Disney Hotels (excluding Disney's Davy Crockett Ranch®) in turn, or dropped at the bus station, near the entrance to the Disney® Parks.

BY RAIL

Eurostar operates a once-daily direct service between St Pancras International, London, and Marne-la-Vallée station, just under a 3-minute walk from the Disney Parks. Journey time takes just under 2.5 hours, making it the most convenient way to reach Disneyland Resort Paris from anywhere in southeast England.

   For information and reservations, tel: 08705 186 186; www.eurostar.com in UK. Additional Eurostar services throughout the day go to Brussels and Paris via Lille, from where you can catch a direct TGV connection to Marne-la-Vallée without having to change in Paris.

BY CAR

Disneyland® Resort Paris lies about 32km (20 miles) due east of Paris at Marne-la-Vallée, a diffusely defined area in the Île de France *département* of Seine-et-Marne. Take the A4 motorway (Autoroute de l'Est, signed Metz/Nancy), which leads to Germany, Austria and Luxembourg via Strasbourg. Disneyland Resort Paris is signed at Exit 14 (take Exit 13 for Disney's Davy Crockett Ranch®).

If you approach from another direction, to avoid the capital, you will probably use the Francilienne (A104 and N104), linking motorways A1 (Autoroute du Nord, bound for the Channel ports, UK and Low Countries), A4, A6 (Autoroute du Soleil, heading south for the Riviera, Italy and Switzerland), and A10 (L'Aquitaine, which goes via Bordeaux towards Spain and Portugal). Follow signs to Marne-la-Vallée (Val d'Europe) until you see signposts for the Resort. French motorways are free of charge in the Paris area.

Parking charges (currently €8 per day for cars; €20 for campervans) are waived for Disney® Hotel guests, who may either park in the appropriate hotel car park, or in the main lot, which holds more than 11,000 vehicles. Note carefully where you leave your car. Each sector is named after a Disney character. Moving walkways speed up the journey from the car park to the main entrances. Cars cannot be left overnight in the car park. If your car breaks down, or you forget where you left it, ask a Cast Member.

Getting around

PUBLIC TRANSPORT

Internal flights Air France operates the majority of domestic flights in France. Daily departures from Orly and Roissy-Charles de Gaulle airports connect Paris with most major French cities and towns in an average flight time of one hour. For information, tel: 08 20 82 08 20; www.airfrance.fr.

RER The Parisian suburban railway (RER, pronounced 'ehr-oo-ehr') links Disneyland® Resort Paris with the city centre. There are five lines (*lignes*): A, B, C, D and E, connecting with the métro and SNCF suburban network.

One branch of Line A4 terminates at Marne-la-Vallée–Chessy (known as MLV for short), just a couple of minutes' walk from the entrances of both Disney® Parks. It takes about 40 minutes to get into central Paris. On your return journey, check the destination board as it's a branched line and not all trains carry on as far as the terminus. Make sure you catch a Marne-La-Vallée train rather than one to Boissy–St-Léger. Single adult fares are €6.30 (children aged 3–11 travel for half price; under 3 free). Trains run from about 5:15am until 12:30am roughly every 10–15 minutes. Consider buying a Paris Visite ticket, valid for 1, 2, 3 or 5 days, if you plan sightseeing.

Métro Paris's underground has more than 350 stations, so you are never more than 500m (550yds) from a métro stop. Lines, numbered 1 to 15, are known by the names of stations at each end. To change lines follow orange *correspondance* signs. The métro runs daily 5:30am to 12:30am.

Buses Buses are a good way to see Paris (especially route 24). Buses run from 5:30am to 8:30pm with a reduced service on Sunday evenings. Noctambus routes depart every hour in the week and every half-hour at weekends through the night. Bus tickets are the same as métro tickets.

TAXIS

Taxis can be hailed if the roof light is on. Taxis are metered with a surcharge for luggage, journeys after 10pm and before 6:30am, and for going from and to stations and airports. Queues can be long, particularly at railway stations.

CAR RENTAL

As an official Disney 'partner', Hertz is the most competitive rental agent for Disney package travellers. If you are staying outside the resort, check other rental firms too (both Hertz and Avis have desks at MLV station, and many others are based at the airports). It's doubtful you'll need a rental car unless you're touring or staying at Disney's Davy Crockett Ranch®.

DRIVING

- Driving is on the right.
- Speed limits: toll motorways *(autoroutes)* 130kph/80mph; non-toll motorways and dual carriageways 110kph/70mph; *périphérique* ring road 80kph/50mph; country roads 90kph/60mph; urban roads 50kph/30mph.
- Seat belts must be worn at all times.
- Check regulations on carrying reflective jackets and warning triangles.
- Random breath-testing takes place. Don't drink and drive.
- Leaded petrol is *essence super* (98 octane). Unleaded is *essence sans plomb* (95 octane) and *essence super sans plomb* (98 octane). Diesel (*gasoil* or *gazole*) is also available. In Paris filling stations can be hard to find.
- If your car breaks down in France tel: 17 for assistance (Police). On motorways *(autoroutes)* use the orange-coloured emergency phones (located every 2km/1 mile) to contact the breakdown service.

TICKETS AND CONCESSIONS

Entrance tickets are sold as 1-Day, 1-Park tickets (allowing entrance to just one park of your choice), or 1-, 2-, 3-, 4- and 5-Day Park Hopper tickets, allowing unlimited access to both Disney® Parks for the relevant duration. You don't have to use the tickets on consecutive days; they are valid for 1 year from the date on the back. Annual Passport tickets are sold in three price-bands for 300, 335 or 365 days. Prices from UK agents vary slightly. Tour operators offer inclusive packages, as well as Disney itself.

Groups of 25 senior citizens (over 55s) or more qualify for a 20 per cent reduction (not always valid during peak periods). Cast members are happy to help anyone with special needs. Carte Senior, valid for women over 60 and men over 65, entitles the bearer to reductions of up to 50 per cent in Paris museums and on public transport. The card costs about €50 for unlimited travel. To get one, take your passport to the Abonnement (ticket) office of any main railway station. The card is valid for a year.

Being there

LOCAL TOURIST OFFICES
DISNEYLAND® RESORT PARIS

The Île-de-France/Seine-et-Marne tourist office (small kiosk) is outside Marne-la-Vallée station and the entrance to Disney® Village.

Espace du Tourisme d'Île-de-France et de Seine-et-Marne

Place François Truffaut, 77705 Marne-la-Vallée, Cedex 4

☎ 01 60 43 33 33; www.pidf.com

PARIS

Office de Tourisme et des Congrès de Paris

25 rue des Pyramides, 75001 Paris

☎ 08 92 68 30 10

www.parisinfo.com

Espace du Tourisme d'Île-de-France

Carrousel du Louvre

Place de la Pyramide Inversée

99 rue de Rivoli, 75001 Paris

MONEY

The unit of currency is the euro (€). Coins are in denominations of 1, 2, 5, 10, 20 and 50 cents, and 1 and 2 euros. There are 100 cents in 1 euro. Notes are in denominations of 5, 10, 20, 50, 100, 200 and 500 euros.

Exchange facilities are at the Main Entrances of the Disney® Parks, and in the two information booths in Adventureland and Fantasyland. You can also change money in Disney Village, and at any accommodation reception desk (if you are a resident). Rates are on the low side and no commission is charged. Remember that you will need your passport if you want to change traveller's cheques.

TIPS AND GRATUITIES

It is not necessary to leave tips in Disneyland Resort Paris, however you may feel inclined to leave something in a table-service restaurant, or to tip a member of staff who has been particularly helpful. Outside the Disney Parks check whether service is included *(service compris)* before you pay the bill. It is customary to leave small change in a saucer at a bar or café. Porters, usherettes, tour guides and taxi drivers all expect tips.

POSTAL AND INTERNET SERVICES

A post office can be found at Marne-la-Vallée–Chessy station, usually open 9–7 daily, but not on public holidays. Stamps are sold at many shops, including The Storybook Store in Town Square, inside Disneyland® Park. There are postboxes throughout the Disney® Parks and Disney® Hotels and Disney's Davy Crockett Ranch®.

WiFi internet access is available at extra cost in Disneyland® Hotel, Disney's Hotel New York®, Disney's Newport Bay Club®, Disney's Sequoia Lodge® and in these associated non-Disney hotels: Holiday Inn, Vienna International Dream Castle, Adagio City Aparthotel Val d'Europe. Free WiFi connection is available in these associated non-Disney hotels: Thomas Cook's Explorers, Kyriad, Radisson SAS. There is no WiFi access or internet café in Disney® Village.

TELEPHONES

Both coin-operated and card phones are available in the Disney Parks, in Disney Village and in Resort accommodation. France Télécom phone cards are on sale at the post office, in shops and at the golf course. Telephone charges are the same in all hotels. They include a mark-up over normal France Télécom rates, depending upon what time of day you call.

International dialling codes

From France to:

UK: 00 44

USA: 00 1

Germany: 00 49

Spain: 00 34

Emergency telephone numbers

Police: 17

Fire: 18

Ambulance (SAMU): 15

SOS Doctor: 01 47 07 77 77

SOS Dentist: 01 43 37 51 00

EMBASSIES AND CONSULATES IN PARIS

UK ☎ 01 44 51 31 00

Germany ☎ 01 53 83 45 00

USA ☎ 01 43 12 22 22

Netherlands ☎ 01 40 62 33 00

Spain ☎ 01 44 43 18 00

HEALTH AND SAFETY

Medical centres First-aid centres with fully trained nursing staff are located next to Plaza Gardens Restaurant in Main Street, U.S.A.® and behind Studio Services in Front Lot. Simple medical supplies can be found in all the hotels. If there is a serious problem, ask your hotel receptionist or the tourist office for advice. There is a pharmacy at Val d'Europe, a medical centre in Esbly and a hospital in Lagny.

Sun advice July and August are the sunniest (and hottest) months. If you're out of doors take the usual precautions.

Drugs Pharmacies – recognized by their green cross sign – employ highly qualified staff able to offer medical advice, provide first-aid and prescribe a wide range of drugs, though some are available by prescription (*ordonnance*) only.

Personal safety Petty crime, particularly theft of wallets and handbags is fairly common in Paris. Groups of scruffy-looking children sometimes work the streets in gangs, fleecing unwary tourists. Report any loss or theft to the *Police Municipale* (blue uniforms).

ELECTRICITY

The power supply in France is 220 volts. Sockets accept two-round-pin (or increasingly three-round-pin) plugs, so an adaptor is needed for non-Continental appliances and a voltage transformer for appliances operating on 100–120 volts.

VISITORS WITH DISABILITIES

Ask for the *Disabled Guest Guide* at the main entrance of Disneyland® Park, City Hall or at Studio Services. The Resort is designed to be user-friendly, but wheelchair users will need to find someone who can lift them out of their chair and on to rides (Cast Members are not allowed to do this). Special vehicles can be provided to help guests reach the Disney® Parks from the hotels, and all hotels have rooms designed for those with disabilities. Parking spaces near the entrance are also available. Wheelchairs can be rented in Town Square in Main Street, U.S.A. or at Studio Services in Front Lot (€7.50 per day; they must not be taken outside the Disney Parks). All WC blocks, shops and restaurants are accessible by wheelchair, and some shops have special dressing-rooms. If you need assistance, enquire at City Hall, First Aid (near Plaza Gardens

Restaurant) or Studio Services. If you have a weak back or neck, avoid the joltier rides. Special aids are available for guests with sight impairments.

OPENING HOURS

Disneyland® Resort Paris can be visited 365 days a year. Officially, the Disney® Parks open at 9 (10 weekdays from September to mid-March) but often they open earlier. During peak seasons, you can usually get inside at least half an hour before the official opening time, though attractions open at the usual time. Weekdays are generally less busy than weekends, and Tuesday is especially quiet. On Monday many shops and other businesses are closed. Schools close on Wednesday, so this is a popular day for French families to visit. Closing times may vary. Although the turnstiles may allow no more visitors if the Disney Parks become too crowded, guests staying in Disney® Hotels always have entry. Check what time the Parks close as you enter: in high summer Disneyland® Park often stays open until 11pm. For details tel: 08448 008 222 (from UK).

GUIDED TOURS

Guided tours can be booked from City Hall in Town Square and Studio Services in Front Lot. They last from 1 to 2 hours. Special tours can be organized for private groups by arrangement for an additional charge.

CHARGES

Prices current at the time of going to press; check before visiting. Children over 12 count as adults and pay full price. Children under 3 can enter free.

1-day Disney Park Entrance Ticket: adult €49, child (3–11) €41
1-day 'Hopper' Ticket: adult €59, child €51
2-day 'Hopper' Ticket: adult €108, child €92
3-day 'Hopper' Ticket: adult €134, child €114
2-Park Annual Ticket: 365-day version €179 (no child reduction)
Car parking: €8 per day
VEA Airport Shuttle: €16 (single adult), €13 (child)
RER to/from central Paris: €6.30 (single adult), €3.15 (child)
Animal Care Center: €8 per day (including food), or €12 overnight
Wheelchair or pushchair rental: €7.50 per day
Buffalo Bill's Wild West Show (Disney Village): adult €59, child €39 (drinks and dinner included).

The story so far

© Disney

The shaping of Disneyland® Resort Paris

The idea of a Disney® Park in Europe goes back more than 30 years, though it was not until 1984 that The Walt Disney Company began to explore the possibilities seriously. The options were wide open. Would English-speaking Britain, whose citizens so eagerly patronize American Theme Parks, naturally play host to Mickey Mouse? Or should the new Disney Park be blessed with that cocktail of sunshine and oranges so successful in California and Florida – by being located in southern Spain, perhaps? Why not target the wealthy Germans? No doubt they could run the show as efficiently as Walt would have wished. Feasibility studies spawned; Team Disney anguished, and then began some hard bargaining. Eventually, the keys to the kingdom fell into French hands. The promised land was a stretch of unprepossessing sugar-beet fields about 32km (20 miles) east of Paris. Not immediately enticing, but the Marne-la-Vallée area had a number of advantages. For one thing, it was available. And there are not that many suitably sized tracts of affordable land available in Western Europe these days. Secondly, it lay slap in the middle of a cat's cradle of important communication networks linking the richest and most densely populated countries of Europe. And thirdly, it was on the eastern outskirts of the greater Paris area. It was, admittedly, a bit damper and chillier than one might have hoped, but you can't have everything.

ONCE UPON A TIME

The Walt Disney Company signed a 30-year contract to develop the site with the French authorities in 1987. The French government purchased some 1,940ha (4,800 acres) of land, a total area about one-fifth the size of Paris, agreeing to release it to Disney as it was needed. Meanwhile, residents and farmers, now tenants instead of landlords, carried on their lives as normally as they could in a region destined for rapid and irrevocable change. Earth-moving and construction equipment arrived to shift millions of tonnes of topsoil into new configurations of lakes, railway tracks, road systems and protective circular ramparts, like some Iron Age hill fort. The statistics were awesome, and the speed at which the project took shape was astonishing. Within four years Phase I of the development was complete, covering 600ha (1,483 acres) of land. The region was transformed, with 450,000 trees and shrubs, artificial expanses of water, and almost 32km (20 miles) of roads. Six extraordinary hotels and a 'trapper village' emerged from the fields, but more curious structures could be glimpsed behind the stockade surrounding the new Disney® Park – a storybook castle, a piece of re-created Arizona and a skull-like cave.

AGAINST THE ODDS

Meanwhile, around the edges of the complex, speculation buzzed, both of the cerebral and mercenary kinds. Rumours of Disney's sinister transatlantic masterplan to undermine 'French Culture As We Know It Today' were fuelled, and many a pundit had a scornful crack at Mickey Mouse.

Not everyone liked the idea of a Disney Park on their doorstep. And, of course, some of the locals had to play the role of dispossessed serfs carefully, to maximize any potential return on their lost land. A crocodile tear or two would not be inappropriate in the circumstances. This controversial climate did not stop entrepreneurs from constructing motels and petrol stations in many of the surrounding villages. These extraneous developments, simply cashing in on the Disney bandwagon, have done most to disrupt the area. Sadly, they are an inevitable consequence of such a huge investment, readily predictable from all the experiences of American Theme Parks.

Other unintentional effects of Disney's impact on this part of France are less tangible, but still worrying. A glance at local tourist literature produces the disconcerting sensation that the whole of

continued on page 42

© Disney

continued from page 39

the Seine-et-Marne region is turning into a sort of giant Theme Park. Many local authorities, spurred to enterprise by Disney's example, are now promoting their tourist portfolios strongly as rival (or rather, supplementary) attractions. Every little sight and mildly pretty village is now paraded before the eyes of Disney patrons like some contestant in a game show. Summer pageants, medieval banquets and candlelit tours abound. With all this going on, there is a strong possibility that some visitors at least, dazed by the razzmatazz, will come to regard the great châteaux of the Île-de-France as mere clones of the Sleeping Beauty Castle.

HAPPY EVER AFTER

For those who recognize the difference, however, the historic and cultural riches of the surroundings (including Paris, of course) must be regarded as one of the most appealing features of Disneyland® Resort Paris. In the US, at Orlando and Anaheim, there are dozens of things to do, but they are an oddly monochromatic mix of Theme Parks and contrived re-creation. In France the texture of the holiday tapestry is infinitely more interesting and complex.

Controversy has now died down as the positive influence of the Disney® Parks on the area's economy is hard to deny. The creation of more than 10,000 jobs at the resort and an estimated 30,000 in

the Île-de-France region, as well as spin-offs for hoteliers and other local businesses, has been most welcome. The infrastructure of the area (road and rail connections, hotel accommodation, and so on) has been boosted out of all recognition. The region was now ready to welcome the Walt Disney Studios® Park, which opened its gates in March 2002, a few days before the 10th anniversary of Disneyland® Resort Paris.

The idea of a second European Disney® Park on the theme of cinema, animation and television goes back to 1992, just before Disneyland® Park opened, but Disney Imagineers were given the green light to begin planning and designing the new Disney Park only in 1997. They based their work on the concept of the successful Disney-MGM Studios at Walt Disney World in Florida and adapted their new creation to European audiences with the help of European professionals in the world of cinema, such as Rémy Julienne, the French stunt designer.

Some agonize, justifiably enough, over the un-Frenchness of it all. There are nods and winks at European fairy stories and children's classics, but basically Disneyland Resort Paris is a heartily transatlantic product, as American as a prime rib steak. French culture, however, is nothing if not robust. The things many people love about France and the French way of life will survive the arrival of Mickey Mouse perfectly well. In any case, before we complain too loudly about the invasion of an alien culture, maybe there are some things about the land of Mickey Mouse that we Europeans should take note of: what, after all, is wrong with clean toilets, courteous staff, efficient transport systems and litter-free grounds?

For the resort to be a success, all Disney needed was for enough people to turn up and enjoy themselves, and then tell their friends. This goal was easily reached, for enjoying yourself at Disneyland Resort Paris is almost unavoidable. Where else can grown-up people ride on an elephant roundabout, or wear mouse ears, without feeling like idiots?

Walt Disney

Walter Elias Disney was born in Chicago, Illinois, in 1901, the fourth of five children in a family of slender means. His father was a struggling building contractor whose varied enterprises consistently failed. When they did, the family doggedly moved on, first to Marceline, then to Kansas City, Missouri. Walt's unsettled upbringing gave him only a rudimentary education, and he spent his spare time living on his wits, delivering newspapers door-to-door and hawking sodas on trains. During a brief stint of ambulance-driving in France at the end of World War I (he was too young to join up), he first exercised his artistic talents commercially, painting camouflage helmets and adding fake bullet holes. After the war Walt returned to Kansas City and found a job drawing for an advertising agency. There he met a talented Dutch artist, Ub Iwerks, and together they set up a company, Laugh-o-Gram Films. It soon went to the wall but, like all true romantics of his day, Walt was hopelessly hooked on the glamour of celluloid. With a small fistful of dollars, he set off to try his luck in Hollywood, followed by Ub. From then on Walt had little contact with his parents. But he always kept up with his elder brother Roy, with whom he later set up in business to produce short cartoons. In 1925 Walt married Lillian Bounds, who lived with his erratic genius for more than 40 years.

After many false starts and financial failures (one of which involved the loss of his prize cartoon character, Oswald the Lucky Rabbit, to an unprincipled distributor), Walt's big break came in 1928, using a new character called Mickey Mouse. The film was *Steamboat Willie,* the first animated film to use synchronized sound. Mickey's squeaks and sighs were Walt Disney's own. Roy Disney attempted to temper Walt's wilder impulses with sensible financial caution, but Walt, always cavalier about the money side, was an incorrigible enthusiast, an ideas man, a risk-taker. And his instincts were sound. He could spot a good story at a thousand paces (and shamelessly borrow it, if necessary) and then would edit it brilliantly for his own medium. Above all else, he was a

© Disney

maniacal perfectionist. Every last detail had to be right. All his life he worked obsessively hard, even coming dangerously close to a nervous breakdown in 1931.

Slowly the Disney studios began to prosper with full-length animations like *Snow White and the Seven Dwarfs*, *Pinocchio* and *Fantasia*. After World War II the Disney brothers seized the opportunities offered by the new era of television. Their Disneyland® programme (set up, in part, to fund the first Disney® Park) was a great success. From animated films, Disney moved on to using live actors in comedies, wildlife pictures and adventure stories like *Treasure Island*. The core of the business was always safe, clean, family entertainment for the post-war era. The films sold like hot cakes.

Walt first dreamed of theme parks in the 1930s, and the Magic Kingdom in California finally opened in 1953. In 1966 his permanent smoker's cough developed a more sinister note, and by December, just a week after his 65th birthday, he was dead – before he could witness the opening of his Florida park.

Few film producers have captured the imagination, influenced so many people, and aroused such loyalty, loathing and passionate interest as Walt Disney. Forty years after his death, debate still rages over the influence of his work – even more over the colossal empire he created to perpetuate it. Through this he has achieved a strangely alarming immortality. So, too, has his single most memorable creation: Mickey Mouse, now over 80 years old.

Mickey Mouse

Mickey Mouse made his screen debut in 1928, in the first sound cartoon *Steamboat Willie*. Created by Walt Disney and originally called Mortimer, it was Disney's wife Lillian who suggested the name Mickey as less pretentious. *Steamboat Willie* was a blockbusting success and Mickey Mouse was soon a household name. He was to become a symbol of American resourcefulness, optimism and energy.

The popularity of Mickey Mouse grew and the 1930s saw his 'golden age'. No fewer than 87 cartoons were made by Disney during that time and new characters emerged who would also become world famous, such as Minnie Mouse, Pluto, Goofy and Donald Duck. In 1940 came the feature film *Fantasia* starring Mickey, with animation techniques way ahead of their time. The stereophonic sound too, was revolutionary.

The world's most famous mouse played his part in the war effort, even to the extent that the password of the Allied forces on D-Day 1944 was 'Mickey Mouse'. During the 1940s and 1950s there were fewer Mickey Mouse films, with other characters coming to the fore. However, Mickey hit the small screen and the Mickey Mouse Club became the most successful children's TV show ever. In subsequent years more children have enjoyed the New Mickey Mouse Club and a third generation of 'Mouseketeers' were seen on the Disney channel launched in 1989.

Mickey Mouse has played a very important part in the development of the Disney® Parks (his first outing was in 1955). He is now seen in both of the US Theme Parks, in Tokyo Disneyland and Disneyland® Resort Paris, where he donned a beret for the opening ceremony.

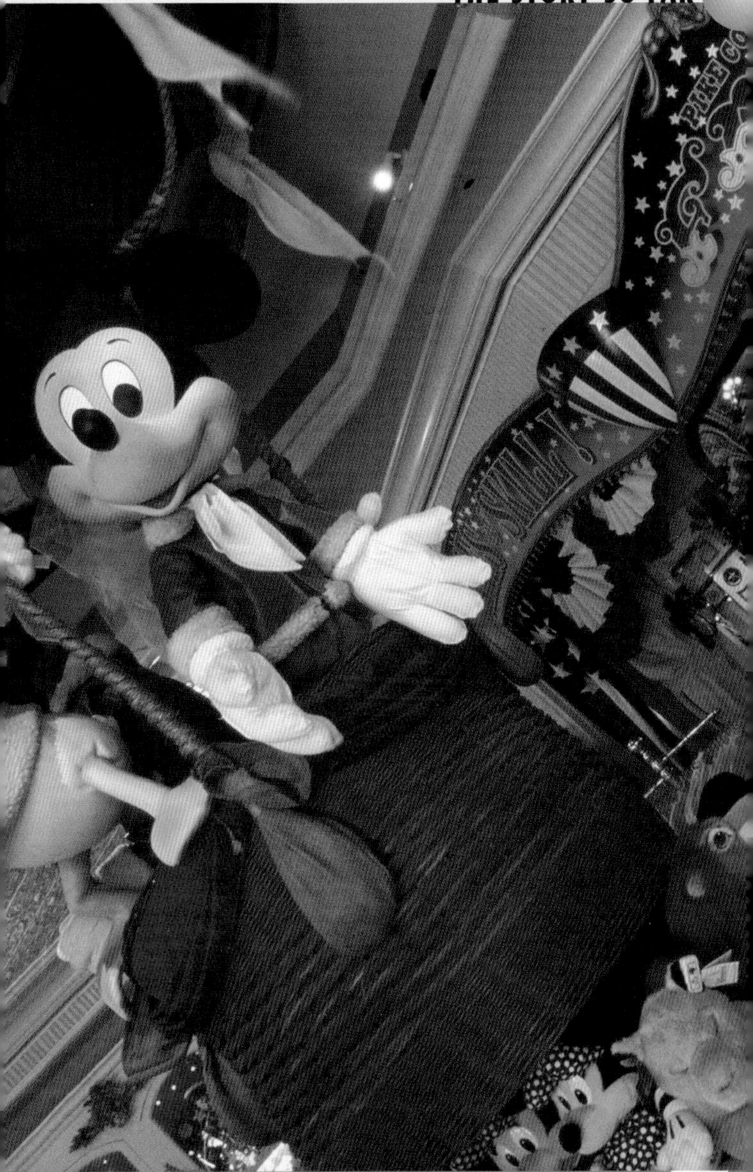

© Disney

Background

In the 1930s Walt began imagining how he could improve on the dreary theme parks he took his daughters to see, but it was only after the war that his obsession developed to fever pitch. At that time amusement parks were bracketed with funfairs and circuses as tawdry and disreputable places. Walt found it very difficult to convey his vision of a place of fun and fantasy in an orderly, civilized setting. He wanted to create a place where both adults and children could enjoy themselves together and come away feeling better. He wanted themes that reflected his Utopian faith in technological progress and the future, a haven in which the archetypal American virtues of pluck and innocence could flourish.

In 1955 Disneyland® Park (also known as 'the Magic Kingdom'), the world's first Theme Park, opened at Anaheim, in Orange County, California. Roy refused to let Walt have the money to build it; he had to cash in his life insurance. But the enterprise succeeded, and the world flocked to see it. Walt began to dream of other Theme Parks, his ambitions growing like beanstalks for a brave new world – a model of planning and innovative lifestyles.

A second site was chosen: the ill-drained acres of central Florida, another 'Orange County'. Quietly the land was purchased on Disney's behalf at knock-down prices through various agencies. Sadly, Walt Disney never lived to see his Floridian dream realized. It was left to his heirs to construct Walt Disney World Resort from the blueprint. This second Disney® Park complex opened in Orlando in 1971, much larger and more ambitious than anything in California.

Twelve years later, in 1983, another Disneyland Park appeared in Tokyo. Soon afterwards, talented chief executive Michael Eisner, recruited from Paramount, was setting a firm course for the floundering Disney empire, which for several years after its founder's death had seemed to lose its way. Throughout the 1980s the Theme Parks boomed, and revenues from television and merchandising soared. By the middle of the decade plans for a European park were firmly on the drawing board.

Disneyland® Resort Paris has undergone a white-knuckle financial roller-coaster since its inauguration, but the mood was confident enough in 2005 for yet another Disneyland to open, this time in Hong Kong. Disney's acquisition of Pixar Animation Studios and the recruitment of its chief executive Steve Jobs (who is also head of Apple Computer) can only strengthen its stake in the worlds of entertainment and communications technology.

IMAGINEERS

Any operation on the scale of a Disney® Park requires colossal planning and co-operative effort, but just how much goes on behind the scenes may surprise you. A whole workforce of Disney employees called 'Imagineers' devotes its time and energy to inventing and realizing the attractions. These artists and technicians are the ones who make illusion reality, working with models and micro-cameras, experimenting with innumerable materials, designs and ideas, studying every last detail for authenticity. It is a serious business: careers have been made and broken over the height of some of the buildings. The complexity of all this is fascinating, though most of the illusions are hidden or barely

perceived by the vast majority of visitors. When you enter Disneyland® Park, notice how far away the castle seems as you look down Main Street, U.S.A.® Why do some of the other buildings seem so accessible? It is all done with clever angles and techniques called 'forced perspective'. Upper storeys are often rather smaller than their proper size, with every architectural detail carefully scaled down. These illusions are just 3-D versions of the kinds of things Disney constantly practised in his films. What the eye sees is not necessarily what is really there, as any animation specialist knows.

AUDIO–ANIMATRONICS®

This Disney-patented system of animating figures (animals, plants, birds and robots as well as humans) has now reached levels of great technical sophistication, and some amazingly lifelike effects can be created. Striking examples of this new technology are the rowdy pirates in the Pirates of the Caribbean attraction in Adventureland. Best of all, without a doubt, is the wonderful dragon that lurks beneath the Sleeping Beauty Castle.

CAST MEMBERS

Anywhere else, these people would be called Theme Park staff. But here they are the cast – everyone from that fellow sweeping up spilt popcorn to Sleeping Beauty herself.

How do they rehearse for that relentless PR exercise, constantly smiling and helpful? They go to university! The Disney University, where appropriate cheerful responses are drilled into prospective Cast Members, and deviant tendencies like tattoos, red nail polish and facial hair are rigorously drilled out. However, some concessions have been made to French fashion: red lipstick may be worn, tastefully. And who are you? You are the guests at this show.

DISNEY CHARACTERS

Minnie and Mickey and the other Disney Character favourites are a popular and ubiquitous feature of the Disney® Parks. They communicate in their own special way, putting the guests at ease, although younger children may sometimes be overwhelmed to meet some of their favourite Disney friends. If you want an autograph, make sure you open the book at a suitable page, and have a pen ready to hand.

Dos and don'ts

Some dos...

- Remember to bring a sweater, light rainwear and to wear comfortable shoes.
- Shoes and shirts must be worn at all times.
- Reduce waiting time by making use of the FASTPASS® service (➤ opposite).
- Children under seven must be accompanied by an adult.
- Make sure you have your entrance ticket with you if you leave either Disney® Park so that you can get back in again.
- Check on closing times.
- Pick up an Entertainment Programme from City Hall in Disneyland® Park or Studio Services in Walt Disney Studios® Park.
- Life is easier if you use a credit card. Visa, MasterCard or American Express are widely accepted. Guests staying at a Disneyland® Resort Paris hotel can ask for a chargecard that can be used within the Resort.
- Visit the tourist office next to the RER station if you are thinking about touring outside the Resort (tel: 01 60 43 33 33, daily 9am–8:45pm).

...and some don'ts

- Since 1 January 2008, smoking in public places has been banned in France. Eating and drinking are not allowed inside attractions and in queuing areas. A picnic area located between Guest Parking and the Disney Parks Entrance is intended for guests bringing their own food.
- No pets, except guide dogs, are allowed to enter the Parks. They may be left at the Animal Care Centre near the car park on production of a certificate of health, or verification of vaccination. A service charge applies (➤ 35).
- Do not leave personal belongings unattended.
- No flash or movie photography is permitted inside the attractions.

© Disney

FASTPASS®

This free time-saving service is designed to cut waiting times at the following popular attractions at the Disneyland® Park.

● Indiana Jones™ and the Temple of Peril, Space Mountain: Mission 2, Big Thunder Mountain, Peter Pan's Flight, Star Tours, Buzz Lightyear Laser Blast.

● If you insert your Park entrance ticket into the machine at the entrance to your chosen attraction, you will receive another ticket for a one-hour time slot later in the day.

● Return during this period, and you can join a priority queue, thus reducing your waiting time.

● Once the time slot for your ticket starts, you can get a FASTPASS for another attraction.

● Obviously there's no point in everyone having a FASTPASS ticket, so numbers are limited, and may run out by lunchtime.

● It makes sense to visit popular attractions as early as possible.

Features of Disneyland® Resort Paris

It is well worth spending some time familiarizing yourself with the layout of Disneyland Resort Paris and the Disney® Parks, particularly if you have only one or two days to see everything. Those hours spent in the Disney Parks will be expensive if you waste time, but if you use them well you will not be disappointed. Study the maps of the Parks, which although not to scale, both show Disney® Village, the parking area and hotels in relation to the Disney Parks.

DISNEYLAND RESORT PARIS

Disneyland Resort Paris covers a total land area measuring one-fifth the size of Paris. When you hear that there is still room for development, you realize the gigantic proportions of the project! At present the resort includes seven themed Disney® Hotels, another seven Selected/Associated hotels and apartments, a 27-hole golf course, the Disney Village entertainment centre, the Disneyland® Park, which alone represents 57ha (140 acres), and the Walt Disney Studios® Park, 25ha (62 acres) at opening stage.

Exit roads from surrounding routes lead smoothly along newly constructed dual carriageways to all parts of the Resort, with all hotels and the main car park clearly signposted from exit 14 of the A4 motorway. For Disney's Davy Crockett Ranch® take exit 13. If you need petrol, you will find it by Disney's Hotel Santa Fe®. From the large visitor's car park (remember in which section you leave your vehicle), covered moving walkways lead to a wide avenue that heads straight for the parks' entrance and ticket offices past the film-set décor of Disney Village on the left. If you have a pet, you must leave it at the Animal Care Centre next to the parking area, where a service charge applies (▶ Charges, 35). At the end of the moving walkways there is a picnic area. There is a car park for disabled visitors nearer the entrance. The entrance gates of the

Walt Disney Studios® Park are clearly visible from the glass dome of the RER station. Spanned by the unmissable Disneyland® Hotel is the entrance to the Disneyland® Park.

If you arrive by commuter train you will emerge at the Marne-la-Vallée–Chessy RER station, very close to the entrance to both Disney® Parks. There is a post office inside the station. Next to it is the TGV-Eurostar station, terminal point of the express link joining several major European rail networks.

Several expanses of artificially created water form scenic vistas within the resort area. Lake Disney® is surrounded by three hotels, each representing a typical aspect of the American scene: Disney's Hotel New York®, Disney's Sequoia Lodge® and Disney's Newport Bay Club®. Two more hotels, Disney's Hotel Santa Fe® and Disney's Hotel Cheyenne®, straddle the Rio Grande, a canal northeast of Lake Disney®. There are traffic-free promenades on either side of the water, making the route between the Disney Parks and the Resort Hotels a pleasant walk, but a free shuttle bus is available. Disney's Davy Crockett Ranch®, situated at the heart of a forested area and symbolizing the American pioneer spirit, is a 15-minute drive from the Disney Parks (no shuttle bus runs).

DISNEY VILLAGE

Opposite the RER station, this startling entertainment complex re-creates the atmosphere of a typical American town: angular metallic structures decorated in zigzag patterns tower above ochre-coloured saloons and bars along a broad walkway leading to the edge of Lake Disney, where a colourful hot-air balloon instantly catches the eye. Panoramagique is the world's largest captive balloon, giving the chance to float 100m (328ft) above the resort for a spectacular six-minute bird's-eye view (seasonal).

During the day the sun glitters on the shiny aluminium and mosaic panels; at night the area is a maze of lights rocking to the sound of live concerts. This bold modern structure,

continued on page 62

continued from page 59

designed by architect Frank Gehry, offers entertainment, eating and shopping facilities to Disneyland® Resort Paris visitors during the day and keeps them happy after the Disney® Parks have closed. It consists of shops, restaurants, bars and night spots, including a nightclub and the popular Buffalo Bill's Wild West Show. It also has a multiplex Gaumont cinema incorporating a giant IMAX screen (English films are shown occasionally), and an indoor leisure centre (NEX) with a bowling alley and arcade games. Additional services include a Travelex *bureau de change*. Just outside the Disney® Village is the tourist office for the local Île-de-France region, and a parking lot with 1,340 places. Disney Village is open daily free of charge, except on one or two special holidays.

DISNEY PARKS

A practical approach is necessary if you want to make the most of the Disney magic. Facilities and services at both Disney Parks are designed to ensure that you enjoy yourself to the full. Bulky articles you will not need during your visit can be handed in at Guest Storage (service charge), situated outside the Disneyland® Park entrance, close to the Guest Relations office, and just inside Walt Disney Studios® Park, next to Studios Service. Note that the self-service, coin-operated lockers just inside the entrance gates of Disneyland Park are no longer in use for security reasons.

Inside the gates, get your bearings as quickly as possible. Look at the map given to you at the turnstiles. Walt Disney Studios Park is divided into four production areas, starting with the Front Lot overlooked by the Studios' Water Tower with mouse ears.

But once inside the Disney Parks, don't be dazzled by the lure of the landmark Water Tower or the enchanting Sleeping Beauty Castle. Instead take time to look around the Mediterranean-style courtyard at Walt Disney Studios Park, Place des Frères Lumières, or the early 20th-century Town Square in Disneyland Park, both of which contain some useful services and facilities.

Disneyland® Park is also divided, rather like a pie chart, into five separate thematic areas or Lands. Beyond Main Street, U.S.A.®. stretching ahead of you lies the park's central landmark, Sleeping Beauty Castle, its spindly turrets thrusting into the sky.

Studio Services (Walt Disney Studios® Park) and City Hall (Disneyland Park), both situated just inside the gates, are the main information centres and are well worth a visit: they are a convenient meeting place for families and friends, and messages can also be left here. Guide maps in several languages, Park information, Entertainment programmes, guide books for guests with disabilities and information in braille are available at the desks. Pick up a copy of the Insider's Guide leaflet, full of useful tips on how to make the most of your visit. You can also book a room, a restaurant, a dinner-show or a Character Tea; check the times of the shows and parades; change your money at bureaux de change; or make reservations for a guided walking tour of either or both Disney® Parks (one-hour tours of Walt Disney Studios Park, two-hour tours of Disneyland Park).

If it's a pushchair (stroller) or wheelchair you need, you can rent one by the day near Studio Services in Walt Disney Studios Park or across Town Square from City Hall in Disneyland Park; a padlock is useful to keep your pushchair safe while you take young children on rides. Note that Cast Members are not available to accompany guests in wheelchairs or to look after children while their parents enjoy attractions that are unsuitable for youngsters. Disneyland Resort Paris has introduced Baby Switch, which allows both parents to enjoy the attraction without having to stand in the queue twice (ask for more information from the Cast Members at the entrance to the attraction). The Lost and Found office is next to Studio Services at the entrance to Walt Disney Studios Park and at City Hall in Disneyland Park.

Before you leave the Town Square to explore the rest of Disneyland Park, bear in mind that this is a good place to watch

continued on page 66

© Disney

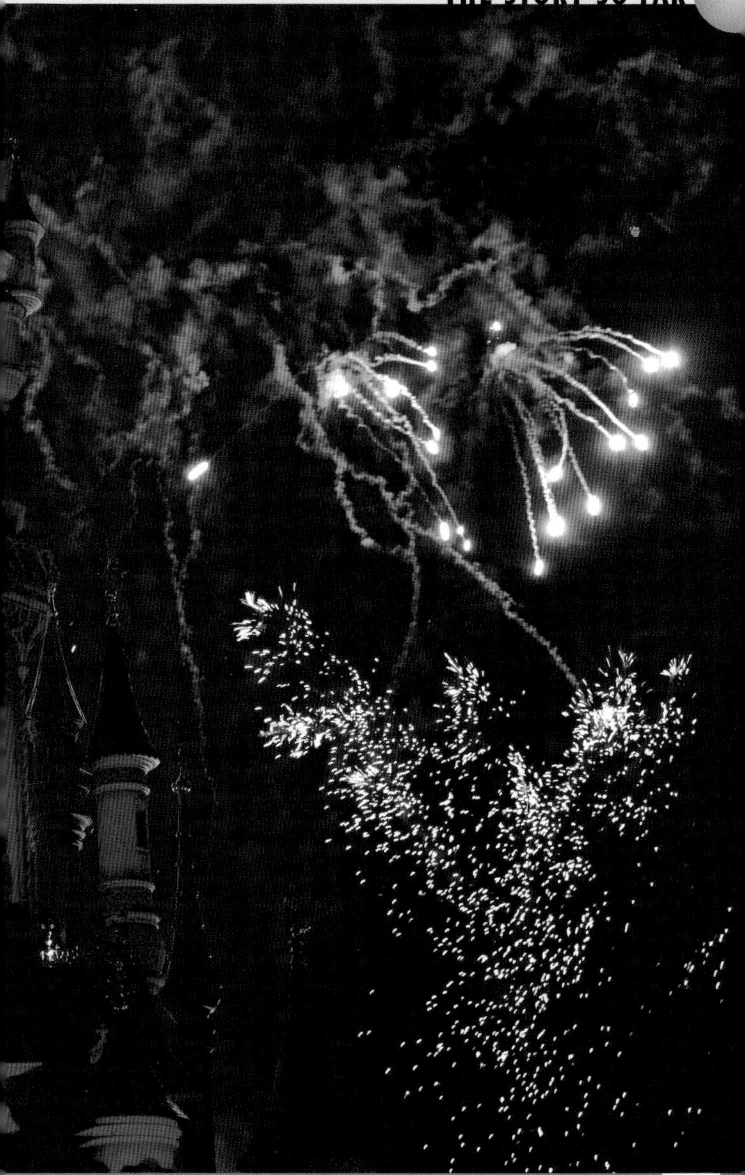

continued from page 63

the Parade and take pictures from different angles as the floats slowly make their way round the square; a spot is reserved for people in wheelchairs in front of Ribbons & Bows Hat Shop.

Now that you have everything you need and are in the right mood, you can uncover the magic of cinema at Walt Disney Studios® Park. Or at Disneyland® Park, you can walk down Main Street, U.S.A.®, hop on one of the nostalgic vehicles bound for Central Plaza or embark on a journey round Disneyland Park aboard one of the steam trains of the Disneyland Railroad. When you get to Central Plaza, you will see the Plaza Gardens Restaurant on your right; next to it are three more services that might prove useful at some time during your visit: the First Aid Centre, the Baby Care Centre and the Lost Children Point. Equivalent facilities are also located behind Studio Services in Walt Disney Studios Park.

If you find yourself running short of funds while you are inside the Disney® Parks, there are automatic cash dispensers next to Studio Services and at Backlot Express Restaurant in Walt Disney Studios Park. In Disneyland Park they are in the arcades parallel to Main Street, U.S.A., in Adventureland and in Discoveryland.

Opening times, operating procedures and so on are subject to change without notice, and it is always advisable to check with Guest Relations for up-to-date information. Occasionally attractions may be closed for technical reasons (such as safety checks) or only open in summer (such as Storybook Land).

MAKE THE MOST OF YOUR VISIT

Your action plan depends very much on what sort of ticket you have. The most popular 'Entrance Passports', as Disneyland tickets are called, are 1-Day 1-Park Passports, allowing access to just one Park, or Park Hopper tickets, giving unlimited access to both Disney Parks for a specified duration. If you have booked a Disneyland package holiday, a Park Hopper entrance ticket will almost certainly be included in the deal.

If you have bought just a 1-Day, 1-Park entrance ticket, you will first have to decide which Disney® Park you want to visit. If you decide to spend the day in Disneyland® Park, you will have to tackle the Park like a military exercise if you want to see it all. Get there early and head for the popular rides first (Big Thunder Mountain or Space Mountain: Mission 2), making the most of slack periods (for example, during mealtimes, the parades or in the evening). You will obviously get more value out of your ticket if you choose a time when Disneyland Park stays open late (in summer, or at peak holiday times). A useful time-saver is the free FASTPASS® (► 57), available at several attractions in Disneyland Park.

A 2- or 3-day ticket obviously gives you more time to experience the Disney Parks. In addition, you can take a rest whenever you want to, and do the things you like best more than once. Remember, you don't have to use your ticket on consecutive days, and if you are staying at the resort for several days, it is a good idea to have a break at some point – see Excursions suggestions (► 154–163). Then come back and have another day at the Disney Parks. Most people can get at least two days' fun out of Disneyland® Resort Paris, and keen theme-parkers will want even longer. Not everyone likes theme parks, of course, so there's a remote chance you may just hate it once you get inside. But there's a much bigger chance that you will want to spend more time here than you have available.

If you do buy a 3-day ticket, do not try to see the whole of either Disney Park on day one. Save some of the excitement for your next visit. In Disneyland Park visit Main Street, U.S.A.®, the Sleeping Beauty Castle, Fantasyland and Discoveryland on day one, and then go to Frontierland and Adventureland on day two. You can try out your favourite rides again, have a relaxing lunch, look round all the shops, or even leave the Disney Parks for a nap or a swim at your hotel on day three. It is particularly important to prevent children from becoming overtired. Particularly if the weather is hot, make sure they get enough to drink and are protected from the sun. No two children react in quite the same way to the attractions at the Disney® Parks. Most take them in a matter-of-fact way, and some are completely blasé, others might be completely overwhelmed by the scale of the attractions. It is quite difficult to assess what may alarm a child. Very young ones may find the spooks in Phantom Manor, the eerier sections of Pirates of the Caribbean, or the Wicked Queen in Snow White and the Seven Dwarfs quite perturbing.

Here is a brief run-down of attractions, showing which ones may suit your party.

YOUNG CHILDREN

Very young children will best enjoy the rides on Main Street, U.S.A®, the Sleeping Beauty Castle and Fantasyland with its fairy-tale theme rides: Peter Pan's Flight, Pinocchio's Fantastic Journey, Snow White and the Seven Dwarfs, Casey Jr – le Petit Train du Cirque or Storybook Land; you could also try your luck with Alice's Curious Labyrinth and 'it's a small world'. Take them for a gentle boat ride round the Rivers of the Far West, and visit Critter Corral to see some real live animals. Make sure they get a chance to meet Mickey Mouse at some point, too. They will probably enjoy the Swiss Family Robinson Treehouse and a ride on one of the steam trains. See the shows at Fantasy Festival Stage, Chaparral Theatre or the Royal Castle Stage. Also, catch the daytime parade, even if the

© Disney

Fantillusion© Parade (on certain dates through the year) is past bedtime.

OLDER CHILDREN

Adventurous types will enjoy Frontierland, Adventureland and Discoveryland, so go to them when you have seen the Sleeping Beauty Castle. After a few rides they may want to try absolutely everything, even 'baby rides' like Dumbo the Flying Elephant and Lancelot's Carousel, but they may scorn Fantasyland's younger appeal at first.

In Walt Disney Studios® Park, Armageddon Special Effects, Moteurs… Action! Stunt Show Spectacular®, Cars Race Rally and Studio Tram Tour® are all suitable for older children; pick up a free programme for the start times applicable during your visit.

A SPOT OF ADRENALIN

Frontierland attractions include a runaway mine train at Big Thunder Mountain and a scary visit to Phantom Manor. Have a go at shooting bank robbers at the Rustler Roundup Shootin' Gallery (you will need extra euros for this). In Adventureland relive the thrills of Indiana Jones™ and the Temple of Peril. In Discoveryland pilot a spaceship in Orbitron®, or take a ride through outer space in Star Tours and Space Mountain: Mission 2. Volunteer for Honey, I Shrunk the Audience, an amazing shrinking experience with visual and tactile effects. In Production Courtyard, the new Twilight Zone Tower of Terror™ is guaranteed to set pulses racing. On summer evenings watch out for the exciting fireworks show called Wishes (selected dates only).

RESTRICTIONS

No children under three are allowed to ride on Star Tours or Big Thunder Mountain; none under one on Dumbo the Flying Elephant, Orbitron, Peter Pan's Flight, Casey Jr – le Petit Train du Cirque and Armageddon Special Effects. There are minimum height restrictions on Big Thunder Mountain, Indiana Jones™ and the Temple of Peril, Space Mountain: Mission 2 and Autopia in Disneyland® Park, and on Rock 'n' Roller Coaster starring Aerosmith and the Twilight Zone Tower of Terror™ in Walt Disney Studios® Park. If you suffer from motion sickness you may be wise to avoid Big Thunder Mountain, Space Mountain: Mission 2, Orbitron®, the Mad Hatter's Tea Cups and Rock 'n' Roller Coaster starring Aerosmith, though an excess of ice-cream is usually more to blame for any queasiness. Honey, I Shrunk the Audience and Moteurs…Action! Stunt Show Spectacular® are fairly loud and intense. If you are pregnant, or have high blood pressure, a weak back, heart or neck, avoid jolting rides.

CHILD FACILITIES

Child facilities are well publicized throughout the Parks. There is a Baby Care Centre in Main Street, U.S.A.® (Disneyland Park) or behind Studio Services (Walt Disney Studios Park) where nappies (diapers) can be changed, bottles warmed and basic necessities purchased. Pushchairs (strollers) can be rented for use within the Parks in Town Square (Disneyland Park) or near Studio Services (Walt Disney Studios Park). There are no restrictions on pushchairs being brought into the Disney® Parks. Lost children will be taken to the Lost Children Point and looked after until you find them. Child menus or child-sized portions and high chairs are available

in most restaurants, and cots on request in all Disney® Hotels
(free of charge).

And if after enjoying a day with the family in the Parks, parents
want to have a night out on their own, all the Disney Hotels
provide babysitting services.

© Disney

Exploring

© Disney

Disneyland® Park

Disneyland Park transmits on a grand scale the Disney magic that has enchanted several generations of children and the young at heart. Here mesmerizing characters welcome visitors to a land where dreams come true, where make-believe is real, where imagination becomes reality. Feel the excitement and laughter as you stroll down Main Street, U.S.A.®, gateway to other themed Lands in the Disneyland Park, Frontierland, Adventureland, Fantasyland and Discoveryland. Through shows, parades and thrilling rides for all ages relive the legendary era of the Wild West, encompass an adventure through the Middle East, African jungles and tropical islands, see your favourite fairy-tales come to life and discover the futuristic sensation waiting at every turn.

© Disney

Main Street, U.S.A.®

©DISNEY

The scene is set by the flamboyant Victorian splendour of the Disneyland® Hotel spanning the entrance gates, even before you pass through the turnstiles into Station Plaza. Once visitors emerge into Town Square from Main Street Station, they are in small-town America at about the turn of the 20th century (as those of us who never saw it like to imagine it might have been). It is a world of gas lamps and horse-drawn streetcars, decorative lettering and absurdly pretty architecture, all in the colours of Italian ice-cream. Each minutely detailed façade in Town Square and Main Street, U.S.A. is different, but the ornate balustrades and bargeboards, pediments and parapets seem to be in perfect scale and harmony. This is a magnificent piece of deception by the Disney Imagineers – the top storeys are subtly graduated in size, so that the Sleeping Beauty Castle appears much farther away than it really is. All the street furniture – lamp-posts, letter-boxes, litter-bins, fire hydrants – have been carefully designed to suit the period.

© Disney

Main Street, U.S.A. is the orientation centre of the Park, where you can ask for information, store belongings, rent wheelchairs or

© Disney

pushchairs (strollers), book guided tours, find out about lost property (or people), and generally warm to the Disneyland® Park mood as marching bands keep up a brisk tempo. The rest of Main Street, U.S.A.® is devoted mostly to shops and eating places. In Town Square there are neat municipal gardens, park benches and a gazebo, where you can board one of the period vehicles to transport you down Main Street, U.S.A., which links Town Square with the hub of the Park, Central Plaza, beside which the Sleeping Beauty Castle stands. From here you can choose which of the lands to see next. If you prefer, you can take a train from Main Street Station, located up steps just inside Town Square, and either go on a complete circuit of the Disneyland Park to get your bearings, or get off at Frontierland, Fantasyland or Discoveryland.

© Disney

ARCADES

There are two covered passageways on either side of Main Street, U.S.A.® with rear access to the restaurants and shops. Inside they are beautifully decorated in fin-de-siècle style, with wrought-iron work and pretty gas lamps. Liberty Arcade, on the left side of Main Street, U.S.A. as you face the castle, contains an exhibition about the Statue of Liberty, with plans, drawings, photographs and the Statue of Liberty Tableau. This is a diorama about the unveiling of the monument – a diplomatic touch by Disney, emphasizing

© Disney

Franco-American friendship and collaboration. The inaugural ceremony took place in New York harbour in 1886. The 33m (108ft) statue by the French sculptor Frédéric-Auguste Bartholdi is made of bronze strips fixed to a steel frame designed by Gustave Eiffel, who made the headlines barely three years later when his famous tower was inaugurated for the 1889 World Exhibition. Liberty was a gift from the French people to the American people to celebrate the centenary of the American War of Independence and French involvement in it. Discovery Arcade, on the right side of Main Street, U.S.A.®, features cabinets displaying various inventions from the early 20th-century flying machines to strange sporting equipment. Fun to look at if you have lots of spare time.

DISNEYLAND RAILROAD

These charming steam engines chug around the perimeter of Disneyland® Park, stopping at Main Street, U.S.A., Frontierland Depot, and Fantasyland and Discoveryland stations. No Disney resort would be complete without an old train or two, for nostalgic railways were one of Walt's abiding passions. He even had a complete track with scaled-down steam engine and carriages built in his garden. At Disneyland Park there are four individual, authentically styled locomotives, all beautifully painted and fitted and evoking the great railroad days of late-19th-century America. One is a Presidential Train of the type used by government officials, another a pioneering Wild West Train, the third an East Coast Excursion Train. The fourth is called *Eureka* as a reminder of the famous cry which echoed throughout America in 1849 and started the Gold Rush. The engines were manufactured by Welsh boilermakers with every detail carefully in place: whistles, smoke-stacks, cowcatchers and shiny brass fittings. These engines genuinely run on steam produced by water going through a diesel boiler, a departure from authenticity deliberately made by the pollution-conscious Disney team. Each engine fills up with water from the Frontierland tank every hour or so. The carriages are open on one side, giving good views of the Disneyland Park. Each train can take about 270 passengers, and one arrives about every 10 minutes; it takes 20 minutes to go right round Disneyland Park. On the journey between Main Street Station and Frontierland Depot the train passes through Grand Canyon Diorama (➤ 88–89).

© Disney

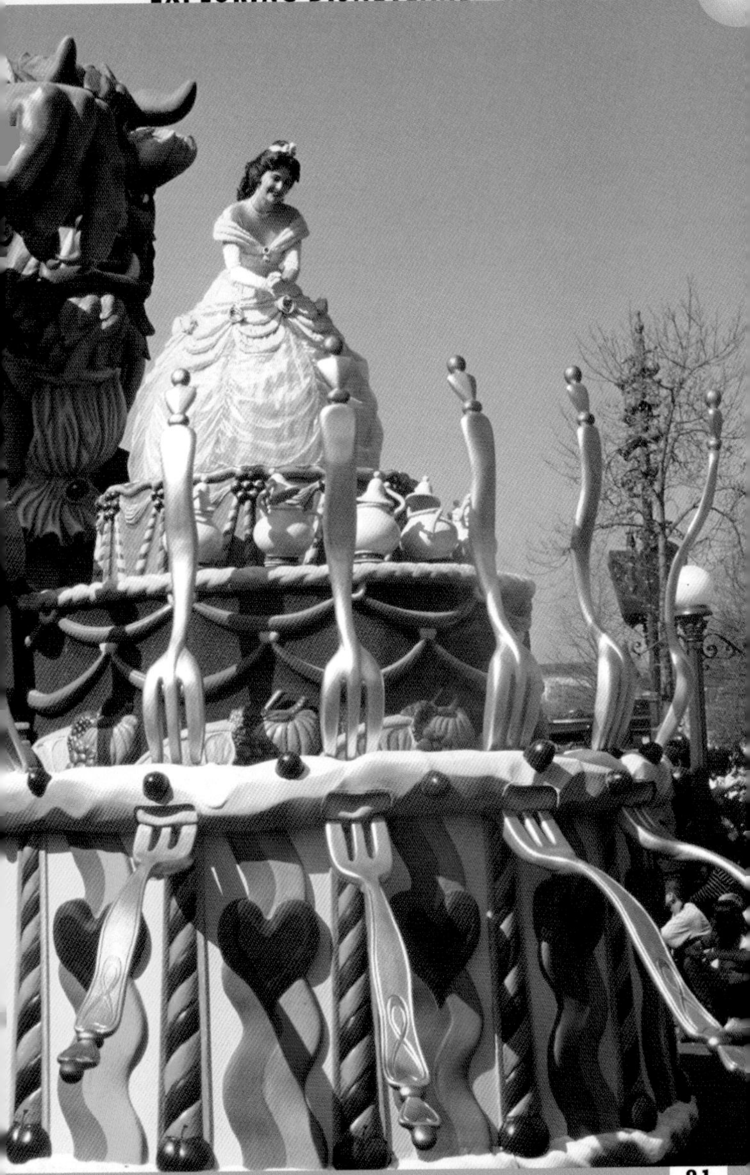

DISNEY PARADES

Disney theme parks are famous for their parades, which are a major attraction and focal point of Main Street, U.S.A.® They are elaborate, colourful spectacles like carnival processions, with lots of floats, lights and music. They generally start near Fantasyland and proceed down Main Street, U.S.A.

You will find the area very crowded. Stake out a good vantage point in advance. An expensive way to do it is to visit Walt's – an American Restaurant. If you are lucky enough to get a window table, you should get a good view of the parades from the upper floor. Views from the other Main Street, U.S.A. restaurants are distant, or will probably be blocked by kerb-side spectators, but you may be lucky in Plaza Gardens.

Traditional daytime parades includes the Wonderful World of Disney Parade©, which draws its inspiration mainly from classic Disney animated films and characters. Seasonally themed parades take place during holiday periods, particularly at Christmas and Hallowe'en. Disney Characters liven up the processions, encouraging young children to join in the fun. On summer evenings when the Disneyland® Park remains open until later, Disney's® Fantillusion© Parade is definitely worth catching for its spectacular floats illuminated by thousands of twinkling lights. Magnificent firework shows sometimes bring the evening's entertainment to a triumphant climax. All shows and parades take place on selected dates only and programmes change regularly, but you can be sure something exciting is going on during your visit.

VEHICLES

Other modes of transportation available in Main Street, U.S.A.® date from the same era as the trains. These vehicles are not genuine antiques, but they are authentically re-created by master craftsmen. Among them are horse-drawn streetcars pulled by patient Percherons, an early double-decker omnibus, a chauffeured limousine, a fire truck and a police wagon. Guests can queue up in Town Square for a brief ride to Central Plaza in whichever vehicle is running. But don't be deceived by Main Street Motors, which in spite of its name and the reconditioned genuine vintage car on display inside, sells souvenirs based on Disney and animated films.

© Disney

Frontierland

©DISNEY

This is the largest of the five lands, distinguished by a Wild West theme, large expanses of water, and a spectacular Arizona-style landscape. Here is one of the most exciting attractions of the Disneyland® Park, Big Thunder Mountain, and a ride on an authentic paddle-boat. Like Main Street, U.S.A.®, Frontierland has a clear architectural theme, based on an imaginary Wild West town of the late 1800s called Thunder Mesa. If parts of Frontierland look surprisingly authentic, that is because they are. Disney Imagineers collected genuine artefacts from many states in the US, and transported them here for special effect.

There is something for everyone here. Even if you are not a Wild West enthusiast, you will almost certainly be impressed by the drama of this artificial landscape, created from unpromising, flat terrain. The Disney Imagineers excelled themselves here, re-creating the American West to such an extent that, looking at the wild canyons and ochre sandstone monoliths, you will imagine yourself travelling through the Rocky Mountains. Pioneer fever will no doubt grip you as you step into the Lucky Nugget Saloon to munch some Tex-Mex and watch a real French cancan show!

You can approach Frontierland from several directions. The usual way is from Central Plaza, through Fort Comstock. If you go anticlockwise, you approach Frontierland from Adventureland, and watch how the pirate scene fades to cowboys and Indians. You can also come by train (clockwise round Disneyland Park). On the way between Main Street Station and Frontierland Depot, trains pass through Grand Canyon Diorama (► 88–89).

© Disney

BIG THUNDER MOUNTAIN *(FASTPASS®)*

The most exciting and conspicuous attraction in Frontierland, and one of the best in Disneyland® Park. It may take a while to pluck up the courage to visit this ride, so wild are the screams from those riding it. But do not miss this experience. It is reached by taking a roller-coaster ride aboard a runaway mine train. The track passes through a reconstructed landscape, similar to that found in Arizona or Utah, particularly around Monument Valley. The rocky set rises to 36m (118ft), and pains have been taken to 'age' the mine buildings by staining, bleaching and rusting.

The ride is certainly wilder than at Orlando. What makes it so good is its mystery factor. Unlike most roller-coasters, the runaway mine train at Big Thunder Mountain is unpredictable and once the train goes into the mine workings anything can happen.

Even the queuing is creatively arranged here – the tightly coiled lines shuffle steadily through the Big Thunder Mountain Mining Company's headquarters. Tension builds up as the point of no return is reached. The train pulls away, then plunges into a shaft and the caverns of the mine workings, full of stalactites and glowing bats' eyes. Hurtling through a mining camp and a pine forest, where possoms swing from the branches, the train dives into a dynamite explosion. The roof caves in, briefly revealing huge veins of gold. The train plunges on, this time facing a new danger from the flooding river, which is washing away part of the track. Eventually the exhilarated passengers are brought safely back to base, eager to do it all again. Children under three (or below 1.02m/3.3ft in height) are not allowed to go on the ride; nor should you attempt it if you are pregnant, or have neck or back problems.

© Disney

CRITTER CORRAL
Enclosure of a typical Western ranch near Frontierland Depot (railway station) where visitors can see and pet some real animals.

FORT COMSTOCK AND LEGENDS OF THE WILD WEST

Guarding the main entrance to Frontierland, Fort Comstock is a replica of the sort of log stockade constructed by early pioneers as a defence against Indian attack. Inside, a series of picturesque scenes depict life in the American West with the help of legendary types of characters immortalized in famous westerns; there is the gold prospector called 'Forty-Niner', because of the 1849 Gold Rush, the outlaw and the lawman, as well as the larger-than-life characters, Buffalo Bill and Davy Crockett.

The Indian Camp outside gives a vivid account of the Native Americans' traditional way of life and visitors can admire authentic Cheyenne handicraft. The tour also offers a splendid overall view of Frontierland and the opportunity to meet a real Cheyenne Indian chief.

© Disn

GRAND CANYON DIORAMA

Although this attraction is located within Frontierland, it can only be seen from the Disneyland Railroad (trains depart regularly from Main Street, U.S.A.®, Frontierland, Fantasyland and Discoveryland stations).

Trains enter an 80m (262ft) tunnel, in which the scenery of the Grand Canyon is re-created, subtly lit to give the impression that the journey along the canyon rim takes not just a few minutes, but an entire day from sunrise to sunset. Guests first encounter ancient Indian cliff dwellings hollowed from the canyon walls, and then a forest in which a herd of deer is grazing. Other wildlife can be seen, too: a fox stalking a pack rat; a rattlesnake coiled on a ledge; raccoons and squirrels; and a cougar and her cubs by a cave. A thunderstorm gathers and, as a rainbow forms, antelope descend into the canyon. The diorama consists of a huge mural, with many animals and species of vegetation. Lighting, music and sound effects all play a part. As the train emerges from the tunnel passengers find they have reached the Rivers of the Far West, with Big Thunder Mountain beyond.

© Disney

PHANTOM MANOR

The eerie, ramshackle mansion of Phantom Manor was built by one of Thunder Mesa's early settlers, who became rich during the Gold Rush. But tragedy struck when his only daughter disappeared on her wedding day. The house was left empty and fell into decay – but isn't that a candle inside?

Guests bound for Phantom Manor are ushered into a strange circular room by sinister hosts. The doors shut and the walls change shape. Those innocent-looking pictures take on horrifying new dimensions as the floor stretches. Guests then descend to

© Disney

board a 'Doom Buggy' for the journey through the house. Mocking laughter, beating door-knockers, creaking hinges, and a clock tolling 13 start the mystery tour. A ghostly bride appears sobbing at intervals, while a medium's head is visible in a crystal ball.

One of the best special effects is the holograms, which are used for the wedding feast. Guests dance and fade, and a parade of ghosts, ghouls and skeletons follows before the passengers are released from their ordeal.

POCAHONTAS INDIAN VILLAGE

This imaginative playground is the perfect place to park young children while you are queuing for rides.

© Disney

RIVER ROGUE KEELBOATS

These boats are modelled on the ones used in a Disney television film called *Davy Crockett and the River Pirates*. They are diesel-powered, 12m (40ft) long and hold about 40 passengers each. The keelboats weave in and out, and you may find yourself perilously close to the rocks at some point. The keelboats leave from a dock at Smuggler's Cove (in summer only, subject to weather conditions).

RUSTLER ROUNDUP SHOOTIN' GALLERY

This is fun. Instead of bullets, the guns fire electronic impulses at a Wild West scene containing 74 animated targets: among them cacti, a windmill and a dynamite shack. (The only human target is a peeping Tom.) If you hit them, all kinds of things happen. There is a charge for this attraction to prevent people from hogging the guns all day.

© Disney

THUNDER MESA RIVERBOAT LANDING (PADDLEWHEEL RIVERBOAT)

From Thunder Mesa Riverboat Landing near the Silver Spur Steakhouse visitors take the *Molly Brown* riverboat. It is an authentic reconstruction of the paddlewheel riverboats that plied the Mississippi and Sacramento rivers at the time of the Gold Rush and was built specifically for Disneyland® Park. The vessel is fitted with mahogany and brass, teak decks and comfortable upholstery. The boat carries about 400 passengers, and the voyage lasts around 15 minutes.

The landscaping and detailing of the sections of the Rivers of the Far West make the paddlewheel riverboat trip round Big Thunder Mountain quite an adventure. On the way you will see Smuggler's Cove; Wilderness Island, a green oasis where Joe sleeps in a rocking-chair, his dog barking at passing boats; Settlers' Landing, a dry dock with supplies for homesteaders; an abandoned wagon with two skeletal oxen in the sand; and Geyser Plateau, where steaming, bubbling, mineral-rich water jets over the dinosaur bones. The scenery evokes a Wild West landscape, with its grand geological formations (rock bridges and canyons) and high desert plateaux known as mesas.

Adventureland

© Disney

©DISNEY

This is one of the most attractive parts of Disneyland® Park. In contrast to Frontierland, here there is no geographic unity since the inspiration of the Disney Imagineers is drawn from three continents – the islands of the Caribbean, the African desert and the Asian jungle. Yet Adventureland is pleasantly landscaped in a natural style, with water, islands, rocks and lots of vegetation, including a bamboo grove. In addition, it has two of the most popular rides, a collection of genuinely interesting shops in its North African bazaar, and several of the nicest eating places. In all, it has a lot going for it, and should appeal to any age group.

One of the two main attractions, Pirates of the Caribbean, is complex and technically sophisticated – yet Adventureland as a whole has an air of innocence about it in keeping with the original spirit of Disney. Its pleasures are simpler than much of Disneyland Park – climbing treehouses, walking wobbly bridges, exploring caves. The central physical feature is Adventure Isle, a moated double-island connected by two exciting bridges. Skilful landscaping gives this area the impression of being larger than it really is. Elements from three well-known Disney movies are incorporated into the themes here: *Aladdin*, *Treasure Island* and *Swiss Family Robinson*.

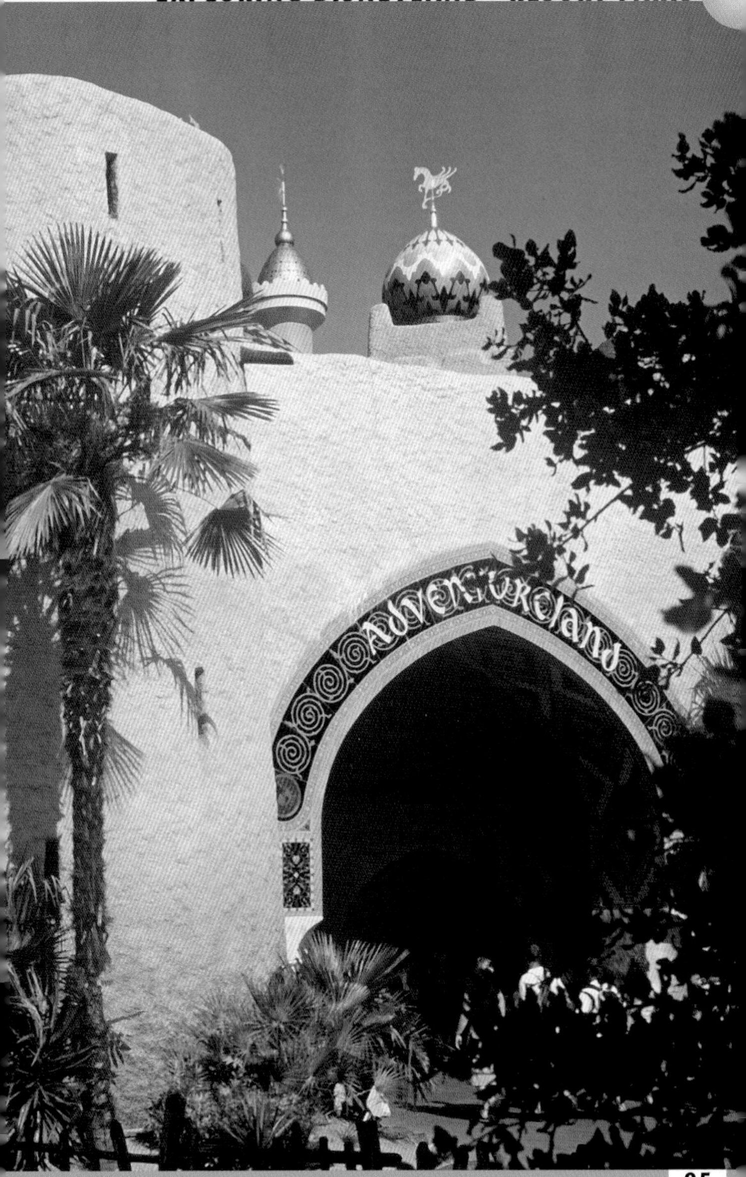
Adventureland

© Disney

ADVENTURE ISLE

The north section of Adventure Isle is given over to a pirate theme.
The Jolly Roger flies by the lookout tower on Spyglass Hill. Below
is Ben Gunn's Cave, with six different entrances: Dead Man's
Maze, Davy Jones's Locker, and so on, leading to mysterious
passages haunted by bats and skeletons. Waterfalls hurtle past
gaps in the skull-shaped rock. Captain Hook's Pirate Ship is
moored in the cove nearby, and you can walk over the top deck to
spy out the land. Down below, light snacks are served from the
galley. At night Skull Rock and the waterfalls are eerily illuminated.
Pirates' Beach is a children's play area (maximum height 1.4m/5ft).

ALADDIN'S ENCHANTED WORLD
(LE PASSAGE ENCHANTÉ D'ALADDIN)

Situated in Adventureland's Bazaar, this attraction brings to life the enchanted city of Aladdin's tales. As you walk through a setting inspired by the Arabian Nights, scenes from Aladdin appear before your eyes, with animated figures and special light and sound effects that will transport your imagination from the city of Agrabah to the Cave of Wonders where the magic lamp lies hidden.

INDIANA JONES™ AND THE TEMPLE
OF PERIL *(FASTPASS®)*

A daring high-speed roller coaster ride culminating in a thrilling loop-the-loop. We all know the fearless archaeologist who appears in several exciting films. The setting here is an ancient temple full of hidden treasures, in a wild, untamed jungle. Aboard a goldmine cart you begin a perilous chase up, over and under the mine site, past ancient statues and teetering columns.

© Disney

PIRATES OF THE CARIBBEAN

One of the block-busting attractions of the Disneyland® Park, a must for everyone. There are similar attractions at the other Disney® Parks, too, but here the latest Audio-Animatronics® technology gives an even wider range of special effects. As you make your way through the rocky grotto to the boats

© Disney

you can hear roistering buccaneers singing their favourite song. You are about to embark on a time-travel adventure, harking back to a 17th-century scene in the West Indies, where palms wave and the air is warm and balmy. The boat sets off through the moonlit Blue Lagoon and gradually the sounds of distant gunfire grow louder; a fortress is being shelled by a pirate ship. Pirates are attempting to scale the walls, daggers clutched between their teeth. The boat then passes inside the fortress. The ride is so packed with detailed scenery that it is hard to take everything in amid the general plunder and mayhem. Passengers can buy pirate souvenirs afterwards in Le Coffre du Capitaine.

As many as 124 Audio-Animatronics® figures are used, including animals. Some of the animated scenes are highly naturalistic and sophisticated: full of sword-fights, facial gestures and so on. The weapons are authentic replicas of 16th- and 17th-century pieces. The dialogue is mostly in colloquial French, but clues are almost entirely visual, so there is no great loss of enjoyment for non-French speakers. This ride is so action-packed that you could certainly do it more than once. Prepare for a few splashes on the way.

SWISS FAMILY ROBINSON TREEHOUSE (LA CABANE DES ROBINSON)

Prominent on Adventure Isle is a strange-looking artificial banyan (fig) tree, rising 28m (92ft). In its branches, bearing 300,000 leaves and 50,000 flowers, is the ultimate treehouse, where the resourceful Robinson family have made a home from shipwrecked timbers. Wooden stairways lead to rooms, while by the roots of the tree is le Ventre de la Terre, where supplies from the wreck are stored behind bamboo bars. (The wreck can be seen under the bridge.)

© Disney

Fantasyland

©DISNEY

When you reach the neat gardens and fountains of Central Plaza, you can see straight ahead of you the mysterious gilded pinnacles of a truly fantastic castle, and the drawbridge is down, just waiting for you to cross. Sleeping Beauty Castle is the main landmark of Disneyland® Park. It is slap in the centre and unmissable, so it is always a good place to meet. Its spires, visible from most sections of the Park, will orientate you if you get lost.

If you approach Fantasyland from Central Plaza when the live show is on at the open-air Théâtre du Château at the foot of the castle, take time to watch as it will put you and your children in the right mood for the fairytale world you are about to enter. You would be surprised how many adults enjoy themselves watching Winnie the Pooh and Friends, Too!. These shows are renewed regularly but are always very popular. Other live shows take place on Fantasy Festival Stage, near Fantasyland Station. Most of Fantasyland's attractions are designed for younger guests; teenagers may find Dumbo the Flying Elephant a little beneath their dignity. At first, that is. The theme of Fantasyland, as its name suggests, is the world of fairy-tales: witches and dwarfs, princes and princesses, ginger-bread houses and magic wishing wells. The European origin of these fairy-tales is heavily emphasized. Architecture ranges from quaint, Bavarian-looking cottages to the ambitious medieval whimsy of the castle itself.

Several of the attractions are similar in type: short rides through enclosed spaces, during which a fairy story is unfurled with many elaborate sets and moving figures. The characters are deliberately based on Disney animated films. There is no attempt to make them look like 'real people'. Queues for these attractions are often lengthy. Pinocchio's Fantastic Journey or Peter Pan's Flight are

© Disney

difficult to follow if you are not familiar with the stories, though you can still enjoy the rides. Other attractions are of the fairground variety – in the form of classic merry-go-rounds and a few mild G-forces. If you know other Disney® Parks you will probably remember the block-busting and eternally popular 'it's a small world', here given more elaboration.

Newer attractions include the hedge maze of Alice's Curious Labyrinth – again, a strongly European feature, and Le Pays des Contes de Fées (Fairytale Land).

Elsewhere in Fantasyland there are many shops selling toys and sweets, and also lots of fairy-tale eating places (designed mostly with children in mind), including one of the few restaurants in the Park with French cuisine, Auberge de Cendrillon. You can reach Fantasyland by the Disneyland Railroad, but after that you must use your feet.

© Disney

ALICE'S CURIOUS LABYRINTH

Based, of course, on *Alice in Wonderland*, this maze of clipped cypress and ivy hedges is 366m (1,200ft) long. You will pass characters and scenes from Alice: the Cheshire Cat, which rolls its eyes and twitches its tail, a blue caterpillar calmly smoking a hookah, strange birds and the choleric Queen of Hearts advocating decapitation at every turn. Eventually you reach a small purple castle, full of optical illusions. The jumping fountains transfix passers-by; arcs of water leap from pool to pool round the edge of the maze. The designs for some parts of this attraction are unusual and keep children amused for quite some time.

CASEY JR – LE PETIT TRAIN DU CIRQUE

Straight out of the Disney classic *Dumbo*, this seasonal circus train rides up and down small hills and over bridges as it jerks its passengers swiftly round the miniature sets of Storybook Land (► 107). A gentle ride for anyone over the age of one.

THE DRAGON'S DEN (LA TANIÈRE DU DRAGON)

Chained by the neck in a dark cave of bubbling pools and stalactites is a leathery grey dragon, wonderfully terrifying. It makes gentle snorings and twitchings, then flashes its red eyes and gives fierce roars, smoke pouring from its nostrils. Its tail lashes in the water, while the wings move and claws tense. It is one of the most remarkable and sophisticated pieces of Audio-Animatronics® technology in the Disneyland® Park. You can reach its lair from the mysterious shop called Merlin l'Enchanteur, carved into the rock of the castle.

© Disney

DUMBO THE FLYING ELEPHANT

The long queues for this ride testify to the popular appeal of this simple roundabout for young children. You can even control the height at which your elephant flies.

'IT'S A SMALL WORLD'

As with similar attractions at Tokyo, Orlando and Anaheim, this is
a very popular and elaborate attraction. In Disneyland® Park it is
a fantastic amalgam of many different architectural landmarks,
ranging from Big Ben to the Leaning Tower of Pisa. The set is
constructed in miniature. Every quarter of an hour a parade of
animated figures troops around the base of the clocktower, and
many exciting things happen before you are eventually told what
time it is. Guests take a ride in canal boats past a gathering of
Audio-Animatronics® 'children' from all parts of the globe.
Norwegian figure-skaters give way to leprechauns, London's
Beefeaters, Flamenco dancers, Balinese fan-dancers and the like.
It is a saccharine show, but the technical effects are none the less
impressive. There are nearly 280 different figures, representing a
phenomenal effort by the Disney costume department.

© Disney

© Disney

LANCELOT'S CAROUSEL (LE CARROUSEL DE LANCELOT)

A classic merry-go-round, with 86 ornate, medieval war horses trotting through fairy-tale scenes. A gentle ride.

MAD HATTER'S TEACUPS

A pleasantly loony whirl in 18 giant teacups, placed on a roundabout, resulting in a bewildering pirouette of motion. You control the speed using a steering wheel.

PETER PAN'S FLIGHT (FASTPASS®)

Pirate galleons 'sail' over the rooftops of London to Neverland, giving an illusion of flight. A delightful journey for day-dreamers of all ages.

PINOCCHIO'S FANTASTIC JOURNEY

Based on the story told by Carlo Collodi. The cars pass from Alpine landscapes into dangers and temptations, and then emerge back in Geppetto's shop, where the clockwork toys spring to life.

SLEEPING BEAUTY CASTLE

This is the archetypal interpretation of a castle – one we instantly recognize from the pages of any storybook, or from early Disney movies, such as the animated classic *Sleeping Beauty*.

The design is loosely based on the architecture of Normandy's famous abbey-castle of Mont-St-Michel, and on illustrations from a 17th-century edition of *Les Très Riches Heures du Duc de Berry*. The building rises 45.5m (149ft) above the moat. A technique known as 'forced perspective' has

© Disney

been employed, to give an illusion of even greater height. The pink walls are topped by 16 whimsical ornamental turrets of subtle, sea-blue tiles. Pennants, weather vanes and golden finials adorn the roofline; creepers hang from the walls; and enticing stairways lead to the central tower. Visitors can enter the castle by the drawbridge, or from the side by the wishing well (Le Puits Magique); don't forget to wish. Once inside, turn and look up at the front window – and

© Disney

wait a few seconds. Magically, its design will transform from two doves into a rose. This is a 'polage window', and it works by means of a rotating filter. Upstairs, in la Galerie de la Belle au Bois Dormant (Sleeping Beauty's Gallery) there is an exhibition of hand-woven Aubusson tapestries, colourful stained-glass windows made by English craftsmen and illuminated manuscripts depicting the famous story of *Sleeping Beauty*. From the balcony, the view over Fantasyland is splendid.

SNOW WHITE AND THE SEVEN DWARFS (BLANCHE-NEIGE ET LES SEPT NAINS)

© Disney

Climb aboard the diamond-mine cars outside the Dwarfs' cottage, and set off through this German fairy-tale, on which Walt Disney based one of his most successful animated films. The wicked queen does her stuff with the mirror and the poisoned apple, and Prince Charming appears at the end.

STORYBOOK LAND (LE PAYS DES CONTES DE FÉES)

Miniature scenes from European fairy-tales unfold slowly as children of all ages take a canal cruise through familiar landscapes that re-create the magical appeal of delightful tales such as *Hansel and Gretel*, the *Little Mermaid* and *Beauty and the Beast*. But there is more...the imposing Mount Olympus where Greek gods once lived, Aladdin's cave and the legend of King Arthur.

Discoveryland

This European version of Tomorrowland also looks back at the great inventors of the past. Here, in France, Jules Verne is given a prominent role; H G Wells and Leonardo da Vinci are also featured.

©DISNEY

© Disney

Special effects form the basis of the Videopolis show and Honey, I Shrunk the Audience attraction. Elsewhere, you will travel through time and space in Discoveryland, and even to the bottom of the ocean in Captain Nemo's submarine (Les Mystères du Nautilus). Certain attractions involve long queues, particularly Star Tours, Space Mountain: Mission 2 and Buzz Lightyear's Laser Blast, although all three benefit from FASTPASS®. Budget-conscious visitors should be aware that the video games arcades (Alpha and Beta) and the interactive computer games of L'Astroport Services Interstellaires (Star Tours Post-Show) are chargeable.

If, as many people do, you tackle the Disneyland® Park clockwise, this is the last land you will come to, and psychologically it feels as though it should be. The architecture is futuristic, with lights and flashing lasers.

© Disney

AUTOPIA

This is a popular attraction, consisting of a ride in a 'Car of the Future' through 'Solaria', a city of tomorrow. Your car is kept firmly on a specific track, and all you have to do is press the accelerator and steer. There's a minimum height regulation for unaccompanied users (1.32m/4ft 3in).

BUZZ LIGHTYEAR LASER BLAST *(FASTPASS®)*

Opened in April 2006, this exciting interactive adventure is inspired by the Pixar Animation Studios film *Toy Story 2*. The Evil Emperor Zurg has a fiendish plan to power up his robot invasion army with the batteries stolen from every toy in the universe. Space Ranger Buzz Lightyear calls on all Disneyland® Resort Paris guests to help him foil the Emperor. Aboard a two-seater space cruiser, you take charge of dual laser pistols and a joystick enabling full 360-degree rotation of the vehicle. Your mission is to shoot as many targets as you can during the ride. As you disembark, your point-score indicates your rank, starting at modest Star Cadet level or achieving the supreme accolade of Galactic Hero. Don't forget your souvenir photo to mark the occasion.

HONEY, I SHRUNK THE AUDIENCE

© Disney

This original attraction, inspired by the two Disney successes *Honey, I Shrunk the Kids* and *Honey, I Blew up the Kid*, opened to great acclaim in 1999. You watch as accident-prone inventor Wayne Szalinski (hero of the two films) demonstrates his shrinking and enlarging machine and commits his biggest blunder – pointing the machine at the audience! From the start you are carefully prepared for the worst as you are given special glasses to wear as you enter the first auditorium, where a multimedia pre-show whets the appetite. You are then ushered into the main auditorium and the action starts, as state-of-the-art special effects create the highly convincing 'shrinking' effect, through 3D visual effects, surround-sound and touch sensations on leg and face. The show reaches its height when young Adam Szalinski picks up the auditorium and the whole theatre starts to shake…

LES MYSTÈRES DU NAUTILUS

This attraction was inspired by Disney's movie *20,000 Leagues under the Sea* based on Jules Verne's novel. Docked in Discoveryland's lagoon, the *Nautilus* is Captain Nemo's submarine, the strange universe of an eccentric visionary who plays the organ at the bottom of the sea. An undersea passage, reached through a nearby lighthouse, leads to the interior of the submarine.

The tour of the vessel holds a few surprises in store for you, as well as some spine-chilling sound and light effects. It begins in the Treasure Room and ends in the Engine Room.

ORBITRON®

There is nothing new about the basic principle of this ride, but it certainly looks different. Bronze, copper and brass globes spin on various axes, the opposite way from the direction of your two-seater craft, so if you are at maximum height (controlled from inside) it seems quite fast. Queues can be very long, as there are only 12 passenger vehicles.

SPACE MOUNTAIN: MISSION 2 *(FASTPASS®)*

Entirely reprogrammed in 2005, Space Mountain: Mission 2 blasts daring 'exploronauts' far beyond the moon to the outer edges of the universe, encountering comets and supernovas en route. This attraction undoubtedly marks the climax of a visit to the Disneyland® Park. The setting, the sounds and the awe-inspiring darkness, torn by incandescent asteroids, are all designed to make you feel like space pioneers. The exhilarating experience begins long before boarding the rocket ship: while you slowly make your way through the heart of the impressive 36m-high (118ft) 'mountain', you experience a taste of the dangers ahead with meteorites and explosions all around. But the count-down to blast off is ticking away and it is time for the rocket ship to enter the barrel of the 22m-long (72ft) Columbiad Cannon, inspired by Jules Verne's novel *From the Earth to the Moon* published in 1865.

The take-off, now from the lower part of the cannon, increases the launch phase by some 40 per cent. Passengers experience acceleration of 14m/s and a G-force of almost 1.3N, before plunging into space on a hair-raising 1km (0.5-mile) journey at a top speed of 70kph (43mph). In its efforts to avoid impending annihilation, the rocket ship makes three complete inversion loops while a sophisticated on-board audio system, with five loudspeakers per seat, adds to the thrills. If you don't want to take the ride, which is extremely intense and has height, age and fitness requirements, you can still gain a vivid idea of this fantastic space journey by walking along the mountain's interior gangways.

© Disney

STAR TOURS *(FASTPASS®)*

This exciting attraction draws on the themes and special effects used in George Lucas's epic adventure, *Star Wars*. As much excitement is created by the build-up as by the ride itself. The sci-fi 'business' before you are actually strapped into your spacecraft, when visitors can

© Disney

watch friendly droids working, is all part of the fun, and certainly takes tedium out of queuing. The attraction is based on a popular comic theme: the novice driver. This one, unfortunately, is your pilot for the space flight. Fasten your seat-belts. The space craft pitches, rolls and jolts, while on-screen, rapidly moving images suggest you are falling or are on some irrevocable collision course. Eventually, of course, you land safely to be greeted by Rox-N, a clever robot who presents the interactive computer games of

© Disney

L'Astroport Services Interstellaires (Star Tours Post-Show) in five languages. There is an X-ray detector with videoscreen projection to eliminate minute space creatures. There is also a sophisticated camera which takes your photograph and projects it on a large screen; you can then distort it at will by dragging your finger across the screen. But the most exciting game is Star Course, when would-be pilots try their skill at avoiding obstacles while hurtling through space at high speed.

VIDEOPOLIS

The airship *Hyperion* marks this pavilion, which houses a large tiered auditorium where visitors can enjoy videos relayed on four giant screens and exhilarating live shows such as *The Legend of the Lion King*. The Café Hyperion offers a good view of the stage, so you can munch hamburgers and hotdogs while you watch. Unearthly special effects are created by lasers.

© Disney

WALT
STU

Walt Disney Studios® Park

Walt Disney Studios® Park, opened 10 years after Disneyland® Park, is designed to take its guests to the very source of the Disney magic, on a thrilling interactive journey behind the scenes to discover some of the secrets of Disney animation, to marvel at special effects, to witness spectacular stunts and take a ride into the Fourth Dimension in the lightning-damaged Hollywood Tower Hotel – if you dare!

© Disney

The park is divided into four Production Zones based on a real studio and includes 12 attractions and several shops and restaurants. There is also endless entertainment called 'Streetmosphere': actors, musicians and characters adding to the atmosphere of a real working film studio. Walt Disney Studios® Park is generally less crowded than Disneyland® Park. Be sure to catch the shows.

Front Lot

Beyond the Park's gates, the inviting courtyard shaded by palm trees with a fountain in its centre (could it be Mickey in disguise?!) reveals none of the excitement that lies ahead.

© Disney

The focal point of this area, known as 'Front Lot' in cinema jargon, is undoubtedly the 33m-high (108ft) water tower topped by Mickey's famous pair of black ears. Originally used to fight fires, such towers became the symbol of a Hollywood film studio; this one was modelled on the water tower erected near the entrance to the Disney Studios in Burbank, California in 1939. And as you might expect, there is a definite 1930s air about the place. Beyond the courtyard lies the entrance to Disney Studio 1.

DISNEY STUDIO 1

Here you step straight into the glaring lights of a Hollywood film set, Hollywood Boulevard, packed with movie props and lined with shops and a restaurant, where guests become part of the action! Studio 1 is a veiled reference to Walt Disney's studios in Los Angeles, which were the birthplace of the Mickey Mouse animated shorts and of Disney's first full-length animated film, *Snow White and the Seven Dwarfs*. Some of the sets are inspired by buildings that actually existed, others help to re-create the atmosphere of Hollywood during the first half of the 20th century.

© Disney

Backlot

According to studio jargon, this area is usually not on show...this is where the tricks of the trade are developed, perfected and eventually filmed, all very hush-hush and definitely out of bounds, but not at Walt Disney Studios® Park!

© Disney

ARMAGEDDON, SPECIAL EFFECTS

This attraction takes its name from the science-fiction film featuring the Mir space station. The pre-show area pays tribute to the inventor of special effects, Frenchman George Méliès, and puts you in the mood for what's in store! Once you step on board the space station, the mounting suspense becomes almost unbearable as all sorts of apocalyptic things happen...or do they?

© Disney

Could it be that those visual and sound effects are more real than reality itself? Well the thrill is certainly real enough anyway, so enjoy it!

MOTEURS...ACTION! STUNT SHOW SPECTACULAR®

This is what every James Bond fan would like to see...a live stunt show! And this is exactly what Walt Disney Studios® Park is offering you – a breathtaking spectacular staged up to five times a day in a 3,000-seat outdoor arena. The scene is a seaside village in southern France, the action: a live shooting of various stunts with purpose-designed powerful cars and motorcycles, and then you get a chance to see it all again...on screen!

ROCK'N'ROLLER COASTER STARRING AEROSMITH

A spine-chilling ride with a difference! It has the speed, the acceleration, the loops, the turns, the drops that you'd expect...but it also has the music and stunning visual effects.

Toon Studio

This is the temple of the art of animation for which the name of Disney became famous worldwide. Five attractions, including exhibits and shows, are devoted to the evolution of animation from its European origins to the most sophisticated feature-length animated pictures of our time.

© Disney

ANIMAGIQUE

Staged in a 1,100-seat theatre, this 'black-light' show using giant fluorescent puppets, ultra-violet light and special effects is partly orchestrated by Donald Duck…with strange results as you can imagine! Characters from your favourite Disney animated pictures (Mickey, Donald, Pinocchio, the pink elephants, the whale…) come to life in this three-dimensional animated show…as if by magic!

© Disney

ART OF DISNEY ANIMATION®

When he visited Disneyland® Resort Paris, before the opening of the new Park, Roy Disney, Walt Disney's nephew (at that time Chairman of Walt Disney Feature Animation), was thrilled by this attraction.

Creating the illusion of motion is a dream that goes back to prehistoric man. Many pioneers have tried to make this dream come true and the pre-show film pays homage to these now-forgotten forerunners. The pre-show area also displays various artefacts, some of them quite unique, such as the multi-plane camera developed by Walt Disney in the 1930s to add depth to animated images by allowing various parts of the same picture

to be animated separately. And why not have a go yourself at the 'persistence of vision' apparatus?

The attraction itself, a sequence which takes place in three successive rooms, includes a film with highlights from Disney's animated classics that will whet your appetite for what follows in the second room, Drawn to Animation: a demonstration of how it is done by a Disney artist with the help of Mushu, the little red dragon from the film *Mulan*. After this, character animation will no longer hold any secrets and you will be given a chance to try your newly acquired skill at the interactive play stations located in the last room.

FLYING CARPETS OVER AGRABAH®

Hang on to your magic carpet as you're whirled round a giant magic lamp and let your imagination take flight into a far-off land where illusion and reality become mixed up.

Production Courtyard®

A statue of Charlie Chaplin as he appeared in *City Lights*, one of his most moving films, marks the entrance to this part of Walt Disney Studios® Park. This is the hub, the place where it all happens, where the spectators' dream becomes reality...on screen!

CINÉMAGIQUE

As the name implies, this show is a tribute to the magic appeal of European and US cinema over the past hundred years. Featuring a selection of the most exciting film excerpts as well as a review of the actors and actresses who are now part of the legend, it invites guests to relive the cinema's greatest moments. Inside the 1,100-seat theatre, do not be deceived by the 1930s décor. The latest technology is here…you are about to experience its powerful effects and witness a disconcerting but exciting fusion between fiction and reality!

STITCH LIVE!

Using up-to-the-minute technological wizardry that has to be seen to be believed, the Imagineers make Stitch, from the Disney film *Lilo & Stitch*, come alive on screen. You can play or have a conversation with him in this real-time interactive experience.

STUDIO TRAM TOUR®: BEHIND THE MAGIC

If you think this is just a tourist ride round the production area with a chance to see what goes on behind the scenes…you're right…well not quite! You will see film sets, props, costumes and vehicles from some of your favourite movies, and learn how special effects are created. Then your tram will take a dramatic detour via Catastrophe Canyon® and from then on you find yourself at the heart of the special-effect shooting of a series of hair-raising disasters!

THE TWILIGHT ZONE TOWER OF TERROR™

At 56m (183ft), this is the highest attraction at the Walt Disney Studios Park. Brave the creepy façade of a once-glorious hotel, board a phantom elevator, shoot upwards 13 stories and brace yourself for a thrilling plummet…

STAYING IN THE MAGIC

Disneyland® Resort Paris has seven elaborately themed hotels, all well equipped. Staying in any of them is a memorable experience that adds much to your holiday. There are many advantages to staying within the Resort; six of the hotels lie within easy walking distance of the Disney® Parks. The more distant Disney's Davy Crockett Ranch® is a budget option designed for visitors with independent transport. Accommodation at the Disney® Hotels is sold as a package deal and includes entrance tickets to the Parks.

In addition to the Disney Hotels, seven Selected and Associated Hotels belonging to other companies lie a little further from the Resort. All have a close relationship with Disneyland Resort Paris. These also have very good facilities. They provide free transport to the Disney Parks, and organize inclusive Disney packages just like the Disney Hotels. Four have been built in a satellite zone known as Val de France, just outside the neighbouring village of Magny-le-Hongre. There's another hotel beside Disney's golf course, and more accommodation at the shopping development of Val d'Europe near Serris (one stop along the RER line towards Paris).

If you are on a tight budget, you may decide to stay right outside the Resort itself, where there are traditional, older-style hotels, and many modern chain hotels at all price levels. It's certainly possible to stay more cheaply here, but bear in mind the cost and inconvenience of getting to the Disney Parks if you don't bring your own car. Several outlying villages are within walking distance of the Resort, or on the RER suburban railway system. Alternatively, you may prefer to stay in central Paris and 'commute' to Disneyland Resort Paris on the RER.

Disneyland® Hotel

This rambling pink confection is one of the most striking landmarks of Disneyland Resort Paris. In terms of bedrooms it is the smallest of the hotels, though you would never think so to look at it. Its florid, Victorian-style gables and turrets, topped with pointed white finials, triumphantly straddle the entrance gates to Disneyland® Park. From Main Street, U.S.A.®, just inside the turnstiles, it is as noticeable as the castle, and many rooms have views of the

Disneyland® Park. The hotel is easily the most Disneyesque of all the buildings in the Resort area. It evokes the grand seaside palaces that graced the smart Resorts of Florida and California at the turn of the 20th century. This is very much a family hotel, with thematic references to Disney cartoon characters. Features include a huge reception lobby, and a promenade, where a piano is played in an elegant lounge. The two restaurants and themed café offer a variety of lavish fare. The hotel also offers Castle Club VIP service with luxurious suites, a private lounge where breakfast is available and soft drinks are served all day, and other additional privileges for an extra charge.

☎ 01 60 45 65 00

Disney's Hotel New York®

If you have seen Florida's Walt Disney® World Resort you will instantly recognize the post-modernist handiwork of the celebrated American architect Michael Graves. His fantasy hotels in Orlando have a similarly extravagant style. Disney's Hotel New York re-creates the landscapes of the Big Apple in a subtle palette of warm terracotta, dove grey and soft salmon. Inside, every last feature of the hotel, down to the Empire State Building lampstands in the bedrooms, echoes the theme. The effect is sophisticated, but fun. It is a more adult environment than the Disneyland® Hotel, and this hotel hosts Disney's lucrative sideline, the convention business (a very large conference centre is attached). Rooms overlook paved plazas or shady gardens and tennis courts. Though it's in the same category, Disney's Hotel New York is slightly less expensive than the Disneyland Hotel.

☎ 01 60 45 73 00 🚌 Free shuttle

Disney's Newport Bay Club®

The irregular, creamy clapboard architecture with the grey-green roofs conjures up a tang of salt spray and a whiff of ozone. This is New England, the Atlantic seaboard. The New York architect Robert Stern designed this elaborate whimsy with classical touches, reminiscent of the Yacht and Beach Clubs at Walt Disney World Resort in Florida. Inside, the atmosphere is elegantly restful in shades of blue and grey. Bedrooms and corridors continue the nautical theme, with porthole windows and ship's tiller headboards. Enjoy an aperitif at the Captain's Quarters Bar or relax in the Fisherman's Wharf lounge. The hotel has its own convention centre.

☎ 01 60 45 55 00 🚌 Free shuttle

Disney's Sequoia Lodge®

Embryonic redwood forests surround the timber wings and shallow, copper-green rooftops of this hotel, bent on re-creating the atmosphere of an American National Park lodge. Décor consists of lots of redwood veneer and grey stone. The main feature of the bar area is a huge, stone-faced fireplace, where there are real log fires. The imaginative swimming pool has waterslides and hot springs, and is one of this hotel's most attractive points. Bedrooms are decorated with wooden furniture and patchwork quilts.

☎ 01 60 45 51 00 🚌 Free shuttle

Disney's Hotel Cheyenne®

A taste of the Old Wild West. Here you will find a life-size stage set of *High Noon*, where covered wagons stand in the streets, and you check in at the Town Bank by the Hangman's Tree. You could be sleeping in any one of 14 separate, wood-framed buildings. The Red Garter Saloon is the place for a drink, but do not expect a peaceful time here. It is very much geared to families, and the atmosphere is cheerfully gregarious. The bedrooms are all cowboy-style, while Fort Apache, in the grounds, is an imaginative adventure playground.

☎ 01 60 45 62 00 🚌 Free shuttle

Disney's Hotel Santa Fe®

We are somewhere in New Mexico at this hotel, marked by a large 'drive-in' cinema screen sign bearing the likeness of Clint Eastwood. A complex of blocks encapsulating the atmosphere of the desert lies behind it, with colours ranging from blues and violets to earth tones. Between the blocks are mysterious sculpted objects, a flying saucer, a volcano, rusting automobiles and giant cacti. The theories behind the architecture of this hotel are complex, and it is worth following the various 'trails' between the buildings that architect Antoine Predock created (the Trail of Legends, the Trail of Infinite Space, and so on). Bedrooms are tastefully designed, using Pueblo Indian themes.

☎ 01 60 45 78 00 🚌 Free shuttle

Disney's Davy Crockett Ranch®

Self-catering cabins. The ranch is about 15 minutes' drive from the Disney® Parks and Disney® Village, south of the A4, so be prepared to use your car on a regular basis since there is no bus service available. However, parking at the Disney Parks is free to guests of Disney's Davy Crockett Ranch. An extensive 57ha (140-acre) patch of mature oak and beech woodland allows visitors to sample an outdoor experience in pioneer style. The luxurious trailer-home cabins have microwave oven, telephone, toaster, dishwasher and a large colour TV, and a maid service every other day. Breakfast is included and can be eaten in Crockett's Tavern or collected and taken back to your cabin. Other features include a small farm of domestic animals, sports facilities (tennis, volleyball, basketball, pétanque), and a swimming pool with waterfalls, bridges, whirlpools, slides and water cannon, housed in a huge, light and airy log cabin. Bicycles or electric golf carts can be rented to ride round the site. An on-site shop provides a wide range of groceries and toiletries, films, sweets and toys.

☎ 01 60 45 69 00

SELECTED AND ASSOCIATED HOTELS
Adagio City Aparthotel Val d'Europe

This well-equipped apartment complex, handy for Val d'Europe's shops and RER station, is ideal for families or groups of friends. Apartments, some duplex, sleep from four to seven people. Breakfast available for an additional charge. The outdoor pool is a bonus.

✉ 42 cours du Danube, Val d'Europe, 77700 Serris ☎ 0825 04 06 08 (central reservations); www.adagio-city.com 🚌 Free shuttle

Holiday Inn

French, country hotel set in a 4ha (10-acre) park with a lake and views across the Grand Morin Valley. This family-friendly hotel is just a 10-minute bus ride from the park gates. A circus theme prevails throughout. The modern family rooms have contemporary artwork and a children's area with bunks, TV and video games. Restaurant; bar; indoor pool; fitness club; children's play areas.

✉ 20 avenue de la Fosse des Pressoirs, Val de France, 77700 Magny-le-Hongre ☎ 01 64 63 37 37; 0870 400 9670 (central reservations); www.holiday-inn.com 🚍 Free shuttle

Hotel l'Elysée Val d'Europe

This modern purpose-built 'boulevard' hotel near the international shopping centre has streamlined facilities. Staff are young and helpful. The RER station lies close by, and the Disney® Parks are just one stop down the line.

✉ 7 Cours du Danube, Val d'Europe, 77700 Serris ☎ 01 64 63 33 33; www.hotelelysee.com 🚍 Free shuttle

Kyriad Hotel

Built in 2003 and styled on a traditional farm from the Brie region, this pleasing complex overlooks spacious, well-kept grounds. All rooms are air-conditioned and can sleep up to four people. Restaurant and two bars.

✉ 10 avenue de la Fosse des Pressoirs, Val de France, 77700 Magny-le-Hongre ☎ 01 60 43 61 61; www.kyriad.fr 🚍 Free shuttle

Radisson SAS

With splendid views over the fairway, this large, comfortable place suits golfing enthusiasts to a tee. All equipment can be rented. Barbecue, family restaurant or fine dining.

✉ Allée de la Mare Houleuse, 77700 Magny-le-Hongre ☎ 01 60 43 64 00; www.radissonsas.com 🚍 Free shuttle

Thomas Cook's Explorers Hotel

This family hotel, opened in spring 2003, has a buccaneering theme. The family bedrooms can accommodate four to ten people and have TV video games. There are two restaurants, a pizza take-away and three bars. Indoor swimming pool; children's play area.

✉ 50 avenue de la Fosse des Pressoirs, Val de France, 77700 Magny-le-Hongre ☎ 01 60 42 60 60; www.explorershotels.com 🚌 Free shuttle

Vienna International Dream Castle

You can live like a king at this imaginary castle, opened in 2004, only a 10-minute bus ride from the Disneyland® Park gates. The stylish rooms have king-sized beds or bunks, and are equipped with all modern facilities. Some have lake views. There's lots for children – playground, splash and fun pool and fairy-tale storytelling – while adults can enjoy the fitness room and spa. Two restaurants and terrace dining in summer.

✉ 40 avenue de la Fosse des Pressoirs, Val de France, 77700 Magny-le-Hongre ☎ 01 64 17 90 00; www.dreamcastle-hotel.com 🚌 Free shuttle

STAYING NEAR THE MAGIC

Acostel

Moderately priced, independent, small hotel with great character and charm.

✉ 336 avenue de la Victoire (N3), 77700 Meaux ☎ 01 64 33 28 58; www.acostel.com

Akena

Budget hotel belonging to the Akena hotel chain, convenient for the Disney Parks; only 15 minutes by car or 10 minutes to the nearest RER.

✉ Boulevard de Courcerin, ZA de Pariest, 77185 Marne-la-Vallée/Lognes ☎ 01 64 62 10 72; www.hotels-akena.com 🚇 RER Line A (10 mins)

Auberge du Cheval Blanc

This small hotel of 22 rooms built in the 18th century promises a touch of Parisian chic. Only five minutes' drive from the Disney Parks. Lounge/bar, brasserie and restaurant.

✉ 2 rue de Lagny, 77600 Jossigny ☎ 01 64 02 24 27; www.chevalblanchotel.com

Campanile

Motel-style chain hotel with 97 rooms, five minutes' walk from the RER station and 12km (7.5 miles) from Disneyland® Resort Paris. The rooms are of a reasonable size and there is a good-value, pleasant restaurant.

✉ 8 avenue Marie Curie, ZAC du centre Ville, 77600 Bussy-St-Georges

☎ 01 64 66 62 62; www.campanile.com 🚇 RER Line A (15 mins)

Château de Sancy

This lovely 18th-century mansion is set in attractive grounds with extensive leisure facilities. There is a swimming pool and tennis courts, and golf nearby.

✉ 1 place de l'Eglise, 77580 Sancy-les-Meaux ☎ 01 60 25 77 77

Golf Hôtel

Friendly place in attractive grounds about 12km (7.5 miles) from the Disney® Parks. The many activities include an outdoor heated swimming pool, table tennis, indoor and outdoor play areas, and access to an 18-hole golf course. Restaurant serving French cuisine.

✉ 15 avenue du Golf, 77600 Bussy-St-Georges ☎ 01 64 66 30 30; www.golf-hotel.fr 🚌 Free shuttle to RER 🚇 RER Line A (15 mins)

Hostellerie le Gonfalon

A quiet, stylish hotel by the River Marne offering luxury in a peaceful setting about 20km (12 miles) from Disneyland Resort Paris. Good facilities.

✉ 2 rue de l'Eglise, 77910 Germigny l'Evêque ☎ 01 64 33 16 05; www.hotelgonfalon.com

Kyriad

This good-value, Swiss chalet-style hotel is approximately 15 minutes from Disneyland Resort Paris. All the rooms have en suite facilities, including bath, hairdryer and satellite TV. Restaurant.

✉ 32 Avenue de la Victoire RN3, 77100 Meaux ☎ 01 64 33 15 47; www.kyriad.com

Mercure, Noisy-le-Grand

Well positioned with easy access to both Disney® Parks
(18km/11 miles) and Paris, and close to the RER and motorways.
The 192 luxury, air-conditioned rooms have internet access and
satellite TV. Other facilities include a swimming pool, sauna
and restaurant.

✉ 2 boulevard du Levant, 93167 Noisy-le-Grand ☎ 01 45 92 47 47;
www.accorhotels.com 🚇 RER Line A (20 mins)

Novotel Atria

Modern hotel with good levels of comfort and standards. The Atria
is located midway between Disneyland® Resort Paris and Paris,
close to the motorway leading direct to the Disney Parks
(18km/11 miles) and a short walk from the RER station. The 144
rooms are equipped with all modern facilities. Restaurant and
swimming pool.

✉ 2 allée Bienvenue, 93167 Noisy-le-Grand ☎ 01 48 15 60 60;
www.novotel.com 🚇 RER Line A (5 mins)

Novotel Marne-la-Vallée

Modern, good-value hotel that opens onto a flowery central
terrace and outdoor swimming pool. There are 195 air-conditioned
rooms with well-fitted bathrooms. About 12km (7.5 miles) from
Disneyland Resort Paris.

✉ Collégien, 77615 Marne-la-Vallée ☎ 01 64 80 53 53;
www.novotel.com

Saphir Hôtel

A modern building set in beautiful gardens, in a small town which
gives direct access to the Francilienne motorway and from there
a 15–20 minutes' drive to Disneyland Resort Paris. The 180
spacious bedrooms are tastefully decorated and well equipped.
Suites are available. A leisure complex has an indoor heated
swimming pool, plus sauna, gym, billiard room and tennis court.
Restaurant.

✉ Aire des Berchères (N104), 77340 Pontault-Combault ☎ 01 64 43 45 47;
www.saphir-hotel.fr 🚇 RER Line A (5 mins)

Tulip Inn Marne-la-Vallée

This elegant hotel with its startling white façade lies in the heart of Bussy-St-Georges, opposite the railway station and 5 minutes' drive from Disneyland® Resort Paris. The 87 smart bedrooms are comfortable and well insulated. The restaurant serves traditional French and Italian cuisine, including great pizza and pasta.

✉ 44 boulevard Antoine Giroust, 77600 Bussy-St-Georges

☎ 01 64 66 11 11; www.tulipinnmarnelavallee.com

🚇 RER Line A (15 mins)

RESTAURANTS

DISNEYLAND® PARK
MAIN STREET, U.S.A.®

Cable Car Bake Shop

Lots of wicked things are on offer in this agreeable (if dark) setting. There is booth seating, decorated with sepia photos of San Franciscan streetcars.

Casey's Corner

For baseball fans. Eat hot dogs and chips beside bats and balls and Coke logos, and beneath Tiffany lamps. You may be regaled with ragtime music.

The Coffee Grinder

Just follow your nose to the tempting aroma and make your choice of fresh coffee and cakes.

Cookie Kitchen

A parting-shot temptation as you try to resist the Cable Car Bake Shop. This counter sells muffins, brownies and, of course, a range of cookies.

Gibson Girl Ice Cream Parlour

Milkshakes, sundaes, banana splits and fruity ice-creams are all here in a pink-and-white candy-striped environment, with girls in frilly dresses and straw boaters.

The Ice Cream Company
Sample your favourite flavour in a cornet smothered with an array of tasty toppings.

Market House Deli
An old-fashioned general store. Sausages hang from the ceiling, and casks and lovely old tins deck the dresser shelves. Munch American sandwiches, such as hot pastrami on rye, and sample turkey and tuna salad.

Plaza Gardens Restaurant
A spacious building beside the Sleeping Beauty Castle, with an outdoor patio. The sparkling, 19th-century, Victorian-style interior is full of columns, statues, stained-glass domes and mirrors. Self-service salads, hot dishes like Maryland crab cakes, and a luscious array of desserts (included in the price of a main course).

Victoria's Home-Style Restaurant
Cosy domestic interiors from the 1890s set the tone for this counter-service restaurant. Eat Victoria's delicious 'pot pies' by the harmonium, or in the conservatory.

Walt's – An American Restaurant
One of the smartest restaurants in the Park. The two-storey building offers elegant table service in nine intimate little dining-rooms, all based on different themes. Take a table inside, or on the outside patio. Classy American food, including Veal Oscar, rack of lamb with goat's cheese, crab cakes and baked, stuffed Maine lobster.

FRONTIERLAND
Cowboy Cookout Barbecue
Tap your feet to country music at this large barn that houses a Wild Western-style barbecue, with inside and outside seating for large numbers. The rustic theme includes agricultural implements, harnesses, quilts, wagon wheels, butter churns and so on, in a hay-loft/grain silo setting.

Fuente del Oro Restaurante

Tex-Mex specials: counter-service *tacos*, chilli con carne and *fajitas*. The building is in attractive New Mexican adobe style, with a courtyard where you can eat while being regaled by the Mariachis, a Mexican group.

Last Chance Café

Last stop before the Haunted Manor. Counter service for sandwiches, turkey drumsticks and beverages. It is carefully styled as a bandit hideout.

Lucky Nugget Saloon

This western-style bar houses a dance show that is shown several times a day and is also a counter-service restaurant. The menu features many favourite American dishes, including spare ribs.

Silver Spur Steakhouse

The smart folks of Thunder Mesa dine here, in stylish 19th-century surroundings, and (needless to say) prime rib steak, cooked the way you like it, is the speciality of the house; the chicken breasts and Mexican specialities are also good.

ADVENTURELAND

Blue Lagoon Restaurant

At the entrance of Pirates of the Caribbean, with a view of the ride. The scene – a Caribbean night, lit by torches, with tropical vegetation all around – makes this a delightful place to eat. Caribbean specialities and fish predominate: snapper, swordfish and other delicacies wrapped in banana leaves. Book in advance.

Captain Hook's Galley

Sandwiches and cakes are available in this galleon anchored off Skull Rock.

Colonel Hathi's Pizza Outpost

Tucked away in the bamboo forest, this makes a pleasant retreat. Built in colonial Victorian style, this counter-service restaurant contains mementoes of many exciting explorations: native masks, a plane propeller, safari gear, hunting trophies and photographs. You can choose to sit on the veranda, or inside – a central sunken dining area contains a great tropical tree where animated macaws and toucans perch; the Charter Room is a stone-built, cosier room with a fireplace.

Café de la Brousse
Situated at the entrance to Adventureland opposite Hakuna Matata, this counter-service restaurant offers a three-course exotic buffet including paella, moussaka, spicy chicken and other treats, all served with rice and mixed vegetables (seasonal only).

Restaurant Hakuna Matata
A counter-service restaurant in an African hut with ethnic animal ceramics, baskets and carvings. Lamb curry and Moroccan meatballs are staples, plus Mickey's fun meal (for children).

FANTASYLAND
Auberge de Cendrillon
Cinderella's country inn is the smartest restaurant in Fantasyland, with beams and a cosy fireplace. Look out for Cinderella's pumpkin carriage in an alcove. Hosts and hostesses wear 17th- and 18th-century costumes, in keeping with the elegant Louis XIV and XV furnishings. The restaurant serves traditional French cuisine. As it is usually very busy it is best to book.

Au Chalet de la Marionnette
This is Pinocchio's favourite restaurant! Fairy-tale frescoes and Tyrolean charm smother this large counter-service restaurant. Chicken and chips, and cheeseburgers, followed by apple strudel, are examples of the sort of fare it offers regularly.

Fantasia Gelati
Italian ice-creams can be eaten outside on the patio. As it's adjacent to the parade route, it tends to fill up at parade times and immediately afterwards, so queues can be extensive.

March Hare Refreshments

Stop off at this strange little cottage for drinks, cookies and brownies. Bright tables are set outside for a tea party.

The Old Mill

In the style of an old Dutch windmill. Snacks of all kinds such as pannini, fritters and fruit tarts, plus soft drinks and frozen yoghurt are on sale. Ideal for tea and biscuits or a hot chocolate after dark.

Pizzeria Bella Notte

Italianate façades set the tone for a feast of pizza and pasta in a setting of hams and garlic. There is also a Bacchic theme of grapes and wine casks.

Toad Hall Restaurant

The expansive Mr Toad invites guests to partake of fish and chips wrapped in newspaper, and roast beef sandwiches at his fine Elizabethan home. The interior is full of *Wind in the Willows* characters.

DISCOVERYLAND

Buzz Lightyear's Pizza Planet Restaurant

This pizzeria is situated conveniently close to one of the best attractions in Discoveryland – Honey, I Shrunk the Audience. There is also a children's play area.

Café Hyperion

The Jules Verne airship, *Hyperion*, is suspended above the entrance to Videopolis. Inside, this fast counter-service restaurant offers salads, burgers and Italian fast food to carry into the auditorium to sustain you through the show.

Chariots Gourmands

You'll find these temporary food carts scattered throughout the Parks, in summer at least, serving a variety of take-away snacks: sausages, bagels, muffins, doughnuts and the like.

WALT DISNEY STUDIOS® PARK

A dozen or so themed kiosks and trucks spread around the Park sell light meals such as hot dogs, pizzas, salads, quiches and chicken wings. There are also sandwiches, ice-cream, pastries, popcorn and beverages, which guests can enjoy while sitting at open terraces.

Backlot Express Restaurant

A counter-service restaurant with a relaxed backstage feel. Club and baguette sandwiches, quiches, salads and pastries.

Café des Cascadeurs

Imagine you're a movie stuntman taking a break at this shiny 1950s-style café serving giant hot dogs or club sandwiches.

Rendez-vous des Stars

Undoubtedly the place to be seen! This art-deco-style, buffet-service restaurant serves international and European cuisine.

Restaurant en Coulisse

This counter-service restaurant on two floors, with pizzas, hamburgers, chicken, salads and ice-cream on the menu, forms part of the glamorous décor of Hollywood Boulevard in Disney Studio 1.

DISNEY® VILLAGE
Annette's Diner

This is a typical 1950s-style diner serving giant burgers, sundaes and milkshakes. Join in with the shoobi-doo and hum to the classic music from the likes of Elvis and Chuck Berry, while waitresses on roller-skates dash up and down and jump on tables and dance to 'Grease Lightning'.

Billy Bob's Country Western Saloon

Shine up your cowboy boots and come on down to this Nashville saloon that resounds with country-and-western music. Enjoy a fixed-price, Texas-style buffet with wine or beer.

Buffalo Bill's Wild West Show

Treat the family to a traditional Wild West meal with all the trimmings. While you eat your cowboy dinner, which includes chicken, roast potatoes and ribs, you can watch Buffalo Bill's Wild West Show. There's plenty of action with horses, a buffalo chase and stagecoach hold-ups.

Café Mickey

Come here to meet some of your favourite Disney characters. Overlooking Lake Disney®, this two-storey restaurant and cocktail bar offers Californian specialities, such as rosemary honey pork spare ribs and a good selection of wines. Don't miss the amazing all-you-can-eat dessert buffet.

King Ludwig's Castle

This large restaurant on two levels is confined within the ramparts of an authentic castle. At King Ludwig's you can appreciate the history that inspired Walt to create his Sleeping Beauty Castle. The menu offers Bavarian specialities, such as *wiener schnitzel* and braised mushrooms with *spätzles* or cream sauce, and it's not difficult to imagine you're dining in the heart of Munich as you sample pretzels in the Octoberfest tradition. Sumptuous desserts include Black Forest gâteau and strudel. There is a pleasant outside terrace.

McDonald's®

This fast-food chain offers no surprises but the Commedia dell'Arte décor is original, and there is a large indoor play area based on the theme of Leonardo da Vinci's discoveries. Located by the Disney® Village marina.

New York Style Sandwiches

An authentic New York deli where giant pickle jars and elaborate speciality bread form the window display. Hot pastrami on rye, cream cheese on a bagel, or a classic bologna could precede Manhattan spice cake. You get substantial side dishes of potato salad or coleslaw.

Planet Hollywood®

A spherical restaurant at the entrance of Disney® Village serving Californian cuisine on a movie set. Look for the famous handprints and memorabilia from well-known movies and their stars. And why not try some of the great cocktails?

Rainforest Café®

The building looks like a mud hut, an appropriate style for the equatorial rain forest, and the restaurant is dedicated to promoting the protection of the rain forest environment. Here you can eat exotic dishes surrounded by wild animals and giant aquariums.

Sports Bar

Watch a non-stop round of televised sport on numerous TV monitors while munching on hot dogs and sandwiches.

The Steakhouse

Prime rib and T-bones are served in a building evoking a Chicago meat-packing warehouse. Classic wines (many Californian) are available, and good desserts, such as brownies and cheesecakes, are served.

DISNEY® HOTEL RESTAURANTS
DISNEYLAND® HOTEL Café Fantasia

A pretty café furnished in pink with a muscial theme incorporated in its décor.

DISNEYLAND® HOTEL California Grill

This elegant dining room has an open kitchen, where you can see Californian specialities being prepared. Lovely view over Main Street, U.S.A.®

DISNEY'S DAVY CROCKETT RANCH® Crockett's Tavern

An attractive log-cabin restaurant, serving traditional American home-style cooking for breakfast (and lunch in peak season) and dinner.

DISNEY'S HOTEL CHEYENNE® Chuckwagon Café
Guests and visitors eat at the Chuckwagon Café, a free-flow
marketplace along Texan lines, where harnesses and bales of
hay deck the high-raftered restaurant.

DISNEY'S HOTEL NEW YORK® Manhattan Restaurant
This slick, smart restaurant is a 1930s experience redolent of
cocktails, dinner-dances and Big Band music, with fine dining in
luxurious surroundings. After your meal you have the opportunity
to retire to the Manhattan Lounge, a perfect venue for after-
dinner drinks.

DISNEY'S HOTEL NEW YORK® Parkside Diner
Eat food from Brooklyn, Chinatown and Fifth Avenue in a New York
atmosphere. A good place to enjoy an evening drink or a casual
(but chic) meal.

DISNEY'S HOTEL SANTA FE® La Cantina
An imaginative Tex-Mex desert café, with gas pumps and
pick-up trucks among the food stalls. An excellent place to
take breakfast.

DISNEY'S NEWPORT BAY CLUB® Cape Cod
From here guests overlook a flashing lighthouse by the shores of
Lake Disney®.

DISNEY'S NEWPORT BAY CLUB® Yacht Club
This speciality seafood restaurant invites you on a gourmet cruise
in nautical-style surroundings.

DISNEY'S SEQUOIA LODGE® Beaver Creek® Tavern
A good place for a relaxing family meal. International cuisine in an
authentic American National Park environment.

DISNEY'S SEQUOIA LODGE® Hunter's Grill
You'll find hearty grills and succulent spit-roasts on offer at the
Hunter's Grill.

SELECTED/ASSOCIATED HOTEL RESTAURANTS
HOLIDAY INN L'Etoile
With excellent views over the Vallée du Grand Morin, this restaurant with a terrace serves international and traditional French cuisine.

☎ 01 64 63 37 37

KYRIAD HOTEL Le Marché Gourmand
Decorated in the local style of the Brie region with stripy market stalls, this canteen restaurant in a separate pavilion serves traditional French country cuisine.

☎ 01 60 43 61 61

THOMAS COOK'S EXPLORERS HOTEL
The Captain's Library
The à la carte menu features cuisine from around the world.

☎ 01 60 42 60 60

THOMAS COOK'S EXPLORERS HOTEL
Marco's Pizza Parlour
Marco's offers lunchtime Italian specialities and take-aways.

☎ 01 60 42 60 60

THOMAS COOK'S EXPLORERS HOTEL The Plantation
Self-service buffets for breakfast and dinner.

☎ 01 60 42 60 60

VIENNA INTERNATIONAL DREAM CASTLE
Musketeer's
Fun family restaurant offering sumptuous buffets with a selection of international dishes.

☎ 01 64 17 90 00

VIENNA INTERNATIONAL DREAM CASTLE
Sanssouci
Dine on a variety of dishes in an 18th-century rococo setting.

☎ 01 64 17 90 00

SHOPPING

MAIN STREET, U.S.A.®

Boardwalk Candy Palace

No children (and few adults) get past this in a hurry. Here there are sweets and fudge, chocolates and toffees of all shapes and hues. Almost behind the scenes, the fudge-makers are hard at work.

Dapper Dan's Hair Cuts

A splendid old-style barber's shop with a striped pole outside; inside among the tiles, mahogany and marble are badger-hair brushes and personal shaving mugs. You can have a haircut for about €18, or a haircut and old-fashioned shave for €30.

Disney Clothiers Ltd

Smart fashion gear sold in a draper's shop, set in a lovely house with a fireplace and velvet curtains.

Disney & Co

A multicoloured air balloon with children's clothing, character toys and gifts.

Disneyana Collectibles

Disney collectors should not miss this shop selling ceramics, jewellery boxes, lithographs and the inked 'cells' from Disney animation pictures. Look for limited edition books and figurines.

Emporium

This is the largest store in the Disneyland® Park and has a lot of souvenirs as well as Bixby Brothers Men's Accessories, selling watches, ties, caps, hats, fancy socks and underwear for the man about town. The old-fashioned pneumatic overhead cash transport system is fun to watch.

Harrington's Fine China & Porcelains

The interior of crystal, stained glass and faux marble sets off a glittering array of glass and china. Watch hand-blown glass turn into animals before your eyes.

Lilly's Boutique
Tableware, crystal items, bathrobes and towels, perfumed soap and hand towels all decorated with Disney characters.

Main Street Motors
Souvenirs and clothing based on Disney and animated films are sold in a setting with a vintage car theme.

Plaza East and Plaza West Boutiques
Two stands on Central Plaza selling Disney souvenirs and gifts.

Ribbons & Bows Hat Shop
Also on Town Square, this shop sells Victorian-style millinery and lots of other things to decorate your head, including hair slides, combs and mouse ears. You can also have your own monogram embroidered for free by means of an old-fashioned sewing machine.

The Storybook Store
Charming little bookshop on Town Square. Disney film classics are retold in many languages – *Peter Pan*, *Alice in Wonderland* and so on. Also available are cassettes, novelty stationery, and Tigger is waiting to stamp your books with a Disneyland® Park memento.

Town Square Photography
Film, video cassettes and other photographic equipment is sold in a setting of an aged photographic emporium decorated with old camera gear. There are also repair and express developing services, and cameras and video cameras for rent. Instant digital processing service.

FRONTIERLAND
Thunder Mesa Mercantile Building
A vast array of Wild West accoutrements, including jeans, coonskin caps, stetsons, cowboy boots and so on, is available at this log cabin. Also Wild Western-style provisions.

ADVENTURELAND
Le Coffre du Capitaine
Pirate gear is on sale in this shop at the exit of Pirates of the Caribbean: pieces-of-eight, cutlasses, eye-patches, skull-and-crossbone hats and flags.

La Girafe Curieuse
Set around a buried Land-Rover, under the watchful eye of a giraffe, you will find safari equipment and clothing.

Indiana Jones™ Adventure Outpost
A tantalizing collection of odd souvenirs from interesting areas: jewellery, shells and the necessities of exploration, such as a watch incorporating a compass.

Les Trésors de Schéhérazade
On either side of the entrance to Adventureland, this outlet offers a selection of brass bells, sandalwood boxes and perfume bottles, and La Girafe Curieuse.

FANTASYLAND
La Bottega di Geppetto
Visit this wood-carver's shop for more unusual toys: children will be delighted by music boxes, cuckoo clocks, puzzles and marionettes, and there are baby clothes.

La Boutique du Château
Within the Sleeping Beauty Castle, this festive shop is a year-round hoard of Christmas decorations.

La Chaumière des Sept Nains
More Disney apparel and stuffed toys, in the cottage of the Seven Dwarfs.

La Confiserie des Trois Fées
Edible goodies in the forest cottage of the three good fairies from *Sleeping Beauty*.

Merlin l'Enchanteur
Within the castle, this shop is hard to resist. Designed as the magician's workshop, the walls are full of intriguing inventions and glittering toys: figurines, kaleidoscopes, chess sets and even a jewelled crown. Everything your child needs to become a real magician and the costume that goes with it.

La Petite Maison des Jouets
Quaint cottage with a multicoloured roof that offers a wide range of cuddly toys and other souvenirs.

Sir Mickey's
A fairy-tale village where Mickey is shown fighting with a giant beanstalk. The two shops here sell Disney mementoes.

DISCOVERYLAND
Constellations
Souvenirs for explorers, hi-tech toys and Disney clothes in a setting with twinkling stars.

Star Traders
All kinds of space-age gadgets and games are displayed in this octagonal building, shaped like a satellite dish: hologram badges, puzzles and so on.

WALT DISNEY STUDIOS® PARK
Legends of Hollywood
On Front Lot, the striking décor here is straight out of a movie, with an array of souvenirs and gifts from beach gear to toy cars.

Rock Around the Shop
At the exit of the Rock'N'Roller Coaster ride on Backlot, packed with a choice of music-themed souvenirs.

Studio Photo
Inside the Studio Services precinct on Front Lot, selling cameras, films and souvenirs.

Walt Disney Art Classics
This interesting gallery in Toon Studio displays a variety of Disney collectables, including Disney Character sketches and cells.

Walt Disney Studio Store
The largest boutique in the Walt Disney Studios® Park, on Front Lot, offers a variety of toys, clothes and souvenirs, as well as a photo development service.

DISNEY® VILLAGE
Buffalo Trading Company
You can get everthing you are likely to need to become a real cowboy here: boots, shirts, hats, bandannas and more.

Disney Gallery
Cinema and art lovers will enthuse at the limited series of lithographs and cells on sale here relating to the latest Disney cartoons. Also china figurines and themed gifts.

The Disney Store
A collection of forms of transport – trains, planes, cars – amid a vast range of 'character merchandise' and clothes to suit the whole family.

Hollywood Pictures
Movie souvenirs (posters, books, photographs and so on), many from the Walt Disney Studios® Park.

King Ludwig's Castle Store
At the entrance to the castle, this souvenir shop sells King Ludwig merchandise such as T-shirts and beer mugs, as well as themed items – swords, shields, dragons and lots more.

Rainforest Café® Boutique
Souvenir gift shop attached to the Rainforest Café where you can buy a memento of your visit.

Team Mickey
Everything you can imagine in Mickey Mouse sportswear fashion clothing and accessories for adults, children and babies.

World of Toys
Children will be fascinated by the variety of unusual toys, games, costumes, jewellery and sweets sold here.

ENTERTAINMENT

Shows
Performances take place several times a day, at Le Théâtre du Château (featuring Winnie The Pooh and Friends, Too!* May–Sep), Videopolis (featuring The Legend of the Lion King*), Fantasy Festival Stage or the Chaparral Theatre (featuring the Tarzan™ Encounter* May–Sep).

Be sure to pick up an Entertainment Programme listing show times. The programme rotates weekly, and most shows last about 20 minutes. The Fantasy Festival Stage hosts performances of music and dancing as well as special events such as Christmas shows like Mickey's Winter Wonderland*.

Parades and fireworks
Disney parades and fireworks are an unforgettable part of your Disney experience. The best include, at Disneyland® Park, the Wonderful World of Disney Parade®* – a fanfare of Disney princes and princesses; Disney's® Fantillusion© Parade*; and at Walt Disney Studios® Park, the Disney Cinema Parade, which takes you behind the scenes of cinema and Disney classics.

Wishes* is the most spectacular display of fireworks, high above Sleeping Beauty's Castle (mid-July to end August) but there are others throughout the year (▶ 82–83).
Shows marked with an asterisk are seasonal and dates may change. Please log on to www.disneylandparis.com for details.

Dinner shows
At present there are two dinner shows, one in Frontierland at Disneyland Park (at The Lucky Nugget Saloon), the other at

Disney® Village. The Lucky Nugget Saloon, all gilded lights and tasselled curtains, is horseshoe-shaped like a theatre, and puts on several 30-minute shows a day. The plot is the corny but enjoyable tale of a fun-loving gal who strikes it rich and heads for Paris, where she encounters Pierre Paradis, the man of her dreams, and collects a dance troupe.

Buffalo Bill's Wild West Show is more expensive, involving stunt riding, lasso tricks and some bewildered buffalo. It is an enthusiastically presented show featuring 'Annie Oakley' (best of the riders), and assorted cowboys and Indians. Based on the touring Wild West Show which wowed France in the 1889 Exposition Universelle, the theme continues to fascinate its European audience. Western-style spare ribs and chilli accompany the show. There is lots of opportunity for audience participation.

Disney® Village

When the Disney® Parks close, there are still things to do. In Disney Village there are a nightclub and bars, shops and restaurants that all stay open late, as well as multiscreen cinemas (including one with a giant screen) that show English films on selected dates.

Hurricanes is the venue for dancing, with 'high-energy' lighting and music, and sunset parties on the veranda (free admission for Disney Hotel guests). Billy Bob's Country Western Saloon has Western music and a Texan atmosphere. Also various live concerts take place on certain dates throughout the year.

HOTEL ENTERTAINMENT

Following the development of night entertainment in Disney Village, hotel entertainment is very low-key these days. However, Disney's Davy Crockett Ranch® and Disney's Hotel Cheyenne® continue to provide live country music and karaoke.

SPORT

BOATING

The excitingly landscaped watercourses of Frontierland, the Rivers of the Far West, which run around that interesting piece of Arizona

called Big Thunder Mountain, provide Disneyland® Resort Paris
guests with an opportunity to take a break from the excitement of
the attractions of Disney® Parks and to cool down on a hot, sunny
day. You can traverse these waters in various craft: River Rogue
Keelboats (seasonal), or a Mississippi-style Paddlewheel Riverboat.
These rides, of course, are free once you are inside Disneyland®
Park, but they are popular and you may have a long wait for them
on days when Disneyland Park is crowded.

CYCLING
At Disney's Davy Crockett Ranch® bicycles are available for hire
by guests staying at the ranch only.

GOLF
Golf Disneyland®
Disney's Davy Crockett Ranch is conveniently close to the golf
course, and it is open to the public. Golf Disneyland® is a
championship course designed to host top tournaments, but
less ambitious golfers of all abilities are welcome. Lakes, hills,
waterfalls, rocks and the most Disneyish bunkers have been
bulldozed from flat fields, creating a series of varied landscapes
that will eventually be sheltered by lush vegetation. Each of the
three nine-hole sections of the course is rated par 36. Facilities
include electric golf carts, a driving range, golf-bag storage and
a putting green (in the shape of Mickey Mouse's head).

The 19th hole has been provided at the circular Clubhouse Grill,
whose windows overlook the putting green. Inside are showers,
lockers, a bar and restaurant, and television room. Coaching, a
repair and rental service, and a shop are also on-site. Test all
aspects of your game in the training area. A range of fees is
available. The course is open every day from 8am (or 9am,
depending on the season) until sunset.

HEALTH CLUBS
The four more up-market hotels (Disneyland® Hotel, Disney's Hotel
New York®, Disney's Newport Bay Club® and Disney's Sequoia
Lodge®) have health clubs with gyms, saunas, solariums,

massage, steam rooms, Jacuzzis and so on. They are free to hotel guests, but a charge is payable for the solarium and massage.

HOT-AIR BALLOONING

PanoraMagique is the world's largest captive helium balloon, tethered on Lake Disney®. Don't miss the chance to soar 100m (328ft) above the Resort for a spectacular six-minute bird's-eye view. On a clear day, you can see some 20km (12.5 miles) around the Disney® Parks (flights are subject to weather conditions).

ICE-SKATING

That colourful ornamental pond outside Disney's Hotel New York® freezes over during the winter months and members of the public can use it during three daily sessions.

JOGGING

There are two jogging trails, one around Lake Disney, and one winding through the forest in Disney's Davy Crockett Ranch®. They are for use by Resort hotel and campsite guests only.

SWIMMING POOLS

If you are staying in Disney accommodation, one thing you should definitely bring is swimming gear. The four more up-market hotels, plus Disney's Davy Crockett Ranch, have their own heated pools. The indoor pools are large and all are imaginatively designed – perhaps the most interesting being the pool at Disney's Sequoia Lodge®, with its rocky waterfalls and woodland scenery. Note that Disney® Hotel pools may be used only by residents of that particular hotel.
Please also note that pools are subject to seasonal closures.

TENNIS

There are four hard outdoor courts at Disneyland® Resort Paris: two at Disney's Davy Crockett Ranch and two at Disney's Hotel New York® (the courts at Disney's Hotel New York are floodlit at night and may be used by other Disney Hotel guests).

There is a charge for use of the courts and reservations must be made. Racquets and balls can be rented on site, but do remember to pack suitable clothes and shoes.

OTHER OPTIONS

If you are staying off-site (not in a Disney® Hotel), or fancy a whole day of sports activities, you can visit an outdoor leisure centre at Jablines, which can be reached from the N3 (exit at Claye Souilly).

● Bus route 24 leaves from the bus station near the Disney® Parks.

● Visitors have access to lake swimming (sand beach), horse-riding, tennis, archery, mini-golf, sailing, windsurfing and more.

● A single modest entrance charge admits you to the centre; activities are extra.

● Groups can stay overnight; there is also a campsite.

● For information about Jablines, ask at the tourist office outside Marne-la-Vallée station.

● If horse-racing is your passion, don't miss the harness-racing at Vincennes with its brilliant flashes of colour-coordinated horses and jockeys.

● Check the publication *Paris-Turf* for race programmes.

Excursions

If your aim is to see a bit more of France during your visit to Disneyland® Resort Paris, there is plenty to do for all the family without having to travel too far. Shoppers will enthuse over the huge Val d' Europe complex on the doorstep of Disneyland Resort Paris. At La Vallée Shopping Village you can find all the latest designer labels – many at reduced prices.

And of course, a short ride takes you into Paris with its fantastic array of smart shops, grand department stores and interesting markets, where you can explore dozens of galleries, museums and famous sights.

In the countryside around Disneyland Resort Paris are several stunning châteaux, some very well known, such as Versailles and Fontainebleau, and other lesser-known gems.

Historic Châteaux

The Île de France, Paris's green belt, is well known for its splendid châteaux and great forests. An hour's drive southwards from Disneyland® Resort Paris will enable you to visit the architectural gems of Fontainebleau and Vaux-le-Vicomte and to explore one of the finest forests in the region. Just to the southwest of Paris is the huge château of Versailles, while on the eastern outskirts of the capital stands the formidable castle of Vincennes.

FONTAINEBLEAU, CHÂTEAU DE

The massive and beautiful château is the main draw, but the great hunting forest that surrounds the town provides a welcome retreat for Parisians. It is an excellent place for picnics, walking, cycling and horse-riding, but is very busy at weekends. As the name suggests, a fountain or spring, now in the Jardin Anglais, is at the origin of this splendid royal residence, which started out as a

hunting pavilion in the heart of the forest. The magnificent apartments were transformed from medieval to Renaissance splendour by François I in the 16th century, and later kings also left their mark.

The opulence of the décor is astonishing, especially the ceilings. The imposing horseshoe staircase decorating the main façade was the scene of Napoleon I's moving farewell to his faithful guard in 1814. In the grounds is the Étang des Carpes (carp pool) with a lovely pavilion at its centre and further on the formal French gardens.

www.musee-chateau-fontainebleau.fr

✉ 77300 Fontainebleau, 63km (39 miles) south of Disneyland® Resort Paris
☎ 01 60 71 50 70 🕐 Wed–Mon 9:30–5 (6 Jun–Sep). Closed 1 Jan, 1 May, 25 Dec ✋ Moderate 🍴 Picnics allowed in the park but not gardens 🚉 Gare de Lyon to Fontainebleau-Avon, then bus A or B ❓ Guided tour, shops

VAUX-LE-VICOMTE, CHÂTEAU DE

Compared with Fontainebleau or Versailles, this château is small, but its moderate size seems only to enhance its attractiveness and means it can more easily be appreciated and enjoyed in a single visit. The interior has many features and fine antiques, but the grounds are most impressive: illusory vistas, neat topiary, canals and terraced parterres. In the stables is a museum (Musée des Equipages) devoted to horse-drawn carriages. Fountains play on alternate Saturdays in summer and candlelit tours are popular.

The château has an interesting story. It was built by the ambitious politician Nicolas Fouquet, in 1656: Le Vau was the architect, Le Nôtre designed its lovely gardens, and Le Brun supervised the interior. After his gorgeous château was completed in 1661, Fouquet made the disastrous mistake of inviting Louis XIV to dinner, to impress him. The king was impressed, so much so that he seethed with jealousy and fury at this social upstart. Fouquet was arrested on a trumped-up charge and his possessions were seized by the king, who commissioned the very same artists to upstage Vaux-le-Vicomte with an even more ambitious project – Versailles.

www.vaux-le-vicomte.com

✉ Domaine de Vaux-le-Vicomte, 77950, 45km (28 miles) south of Disneyland® Resort Paris ☎ 01 64 14 41 90 🕐 Late Mar to mid-Nov Mon–Fri 10–1, 2–6, Sat–Sun 10–6 🍽 Moderate 🍴 Restaurant (€), picnic area
🚃 Gare de Lyon to Melun then taxi; shuttle bus at weekends/public hols
❓ Shop

VERSAILLES, CHÂTEAU DE

Versailles is the ultimate symbol of French grandeur, and the backdrop to the death of the French monarchy. In 1661, when Louis XIV announced his intention of moving his court to this deserted swamp, it was to create a royal residence, seat of government and home to French nobility. Construction continued until his death in 1715, by which time the 100ha (247-acre) park had been tamed to perfection by renowned landscape garden designer André Le Nôtre. Hundreds of statues, follies and spectacular fountains, and the royal retreats of the Grand and Petit Trianon relieve the formal symmetry, while rowing boats, bicycles and a minitrain now offer a diversion from the wealth of history. The castle is huge (680m/2,230ft long) and it is impossible to see everything in the course of one visit. Aim for the first floor with the Grands Appartements (State Apartments), which include the staggeringly ornate Hall of Mirrors. The Petits Appartements display France's most priceless examples of 18th-century decoration and may be visited by guided tour only.

www.chateauversailles.fr

✉ Château de Versailles, 78000 Versailles, 20km (12.5 miles) southwest of Paris ☎ 0810 811 614 🕐 Château: Tue–Sun 9–5:30 (6:30 in summer). Parc: 8–6 (up to 8:30 depending on season) 💶 Expensive 🍴 Café (€); restaurant (€€) 🚉 Gare St-Lazare to Versailles Rive Droit ❓ Guided tours, shops

VINCENNES, CHÂTEAU DE

This austere castle, on the eastern outskirts of Paris, was a royal residence from the Middle Ages to the mid-17th century. Inside the defensive wall there are in fact two castles: the 50m-high (164ft) keep built in the 14th century; and the two classical pavilions (Le Pavillon du Reine and Le Pavillon du Roi) built by Le Vau for Cardinal Mazarin in 1652.

www.chateau-vincennes.com

✉ Avenue de Paris, 94300 Vincennes, 6km (4 miles) east of Paris

☎ 01 48 08 31 20

🕐 Daily 10–5 (6 in summer). Closed 1 May, 1 Nov, 11 Nov, 25 Dec

👋 Inexpensive

🚇 Vincennes

❓ Guided tours, shop

VAL D'EUROPE

If you need a change of scene from the Disney universe, this purpose-built development just one stop up the RER Line A towards Paris is well worth a visit.

A couple of minutes' walk from the RER station stands a huge glass-and-metal complex offering shopping, eating and entertainment. The International Shopping Centre is a double-decker indoor mall incorporating an Auchan hypermarket, plus around 130 separate shops selling a wide range of clothing, electronics, housewares, sports goods and more.

Beyond it lies an attractively designed 'outlet shopping village' called La Vallée, consisting of more than 70 designer boutiques selling previous-season and end-of-line stock at prices discounted by up to a third. Well-known international labels include Armani, Burberry, Charles Tyrwhitt, Cacherel, etc. There are plenty of eating places at Val d'Europe, and a branch of the splendid boulangerie/pâtisserie Paul does a brisk trade. The centre is open 7 days a week.

Val d'Europe also has a **Sea Life** aquarium displaying a fascinating world of exotic marine creatures in more than 30 separate tanks. You can walk through a 360-degree underwater tunnel, and enjoy close encounters with giant sting-rays in the touch-pools. It runs energetic breeding and conservation programmes to protect endangered species such as sea horses and sharks, and campaigns to draw attention to the threat of overfishing in the world's oceans.

Sea Life Val d'Europe

www.sealifeeurope.com

✉ Centre Commercial Val d'Europe, 14 cours du Danube, Serris 77711, Marne-la-Vallée ☎ 01 60 42 33 66 ⊙ Daily 10–5:30 🖐 Moderate 🚇 RER Line A Val d'Europe ❓ Free parking, shop

HOTELS

FONTAINEBLEAU

🚋 Gare de Lyon to Fontainebleau-Avon then 🚌 A or B

Hôtel l'Aigle Noir (€€€)

Napoleon III-style decoration is prominent at this hotel facing
the castle; fitness club, indoor swimming pool and a very
good restaurant.

✉ 27 place Napoléon Bonaparte, 77300 Fontainebleau ☎ 01 60 74 60 00;
www.hotelaiglenoir.fr

Hôtel Le Richelieu (€)

Reasonably priced yet comfortable hotel, one of the Logis de
France traditional establishments.

✉ 4 rue Richelieu, 77300 Fontainebleau ☎ 01 64 22 26 46

Victoria (€–€€)

This historic building is the former home of French novelist George
Sand. The rooms have been refurbished, some overlooking the
tranquil gardens.

✉ 112 rue de France, 77300 Fontainebleau ☎ 01 60 74 90 00;
www.hotelvictoria.com

AROUND THE FORÊT DE FONTAINEBLEAU
BARBIZON

Auberge Les Alouettes (€€)

A 19th-century building with rustic décor and extensive, shady
gardens, away from the main street. Delightful restaurant serving
interesting French cuisine.

✉ 4 rue Antoine-Barye, 77630 Barbizon ☎ 01 60 66 41 98

Hostellerie de la Clé d'Or (€)

A former coaching-inn with bedrooms overlooking the peaceful
garden. There is an attractive terrace for enjoying summer meals
out of doors.

✉ 73 Grande-Rue, 77630 Barbizon ☎ 01 60 66 40 96;
www.hotelcledor.com

Hôtel Les Charmettes (€)

Picturesque, timber-framed Logis de France hotel. Amenities
include a restaurant, a bar and garden terrace.

✉ 40 Grande-Rue, 77630 Barbizon ☎ 01 60 66 40 21

Hôtellerie du Bas Bréau (€€€)

A Relais et Châteaux establishment set in beautiful gardens –
previous guests include Robert Louis Stevenson. Luxurious
accommodation and fine dining.

✉ 22 Grande Rue, 77630 Barbizon ☎ 01 60 66 40 05; www.bas-breau.com

VERSAILLES

🚉 Gare St-Lazare to Versailles Rive Droite; RER C to Versailles Rive Gauche

Home St-Louis (€)

A quiet, family-run place in the attractive St-Louis district not far
from the château. It has a cared-for atmosphere; excellent value.

✉ 28 rue St-Louis, 78000 Versailles ☎ 01 39 50 23 55;
www.lehomestlouis.com

Pullman Château de Versailles (€€€)

Luxury château hotel next to Château de Versailles.

✉ 2 bis avenue de Paris, 78000 Versailles ☎ 01 39 07 46 46;
www.accorhotels.com

Relais de Courlande (€€)

Attractive, converted, 16th-century farmhouse with hydrotherapy
facilities.

✉ 23 rue de la Division Leclerc, 78350 Les Loges-en-Josas
☎ 01 30 83 84 00; www.relais-de-courlande.com

Trianon Palace (€€€)

This luxury establishment, on the edge of the Parc de Versailles,
boasts an exclusive fitness club, two tennis courts, and golf and
horse-riding facilities.

✉ 1 boulevard de la Reine, 78000 Versailles ☎ 01 30 84 50 00;
www.starwoodhotels.com

RESTAURANTS

FONTAINEBLEAU

🚉 Gare de Lyon to Fontainebleau-Avon then 🚌 A or B

L'Atrium (€–€€)

Pizzeria in the town centre; with attractive year-round terrace dining.

✉ 20 rue France, 77300 Fontainebleau ☎ 01 64 22 18 36
🕐 Lunch, dinner

Le Montijo (€€)

Brasserie in a luxury hotel (➤ 164) facing the château; terrace in summer.

✉ Hôtel l'Aigle Noir, 27 place Napoléon Bonaparte, 77300 Fontainebleau
☎ 01 60 74 60 00 🕐 Lunch, dinner

Le Caveau des Ducs (€€)

Elegant restaurant in vaulted cellars; terrace in summer.

✉ 24 rue Ferrare, 77300 Fontainebleau ☎ 01 64 22 05 05
🕐 Lunch, dinner

AROUND THE FORÊT DE FONTAINEBLEAU
BARBIZON

L'Angélus (€€)

Convivial gastronomic restaurant with a terrace in summer.

✉ 31 Grande-Rue, 77630 Barbizon ☎ 01 60 66 40 30 🕐 Lunch, dinner;
closed Mon, Tue

VAUX-LE-VICOMTE

🚉 Gare de Lyon to Melun

L'Ecureuil (€–€€)

This self-service cafeteria beside the château entrance is housed in a rather grand converted barn. Steaks, snacks and coffee take on new dimensions beneath the imposing rafters.

✉ Château de Vaux-le-Vicomte, 77950 ☎ 01 60 66 95 66 🕐 Lunch and tea daily; dinner during candlelit visits (see château times ➤ 159)

VERSAILLES
🚉 Gare St-Lazare to Versailles Rive Droite; RER C to Versailles Rive Gauche

Le Boeuf à la Mode (€)
Old-fashioned brasserie with sunny terrace serving excellent duck and vegetable spaghettis.
✉ 4 rue du Pain, 78000 Versailles ☎ 01 39 50 31 99 🕐 Lunch, dinner

L'Harmonium (€–€€)
Food from around the world is served in a modern and refined style, a few steps away from the château. Terrace.
✉ 64 rue d'Anjou, 78000 Versailles ☎ 01 39 25 00 88 🕐 Lunch, dinner; closed Sun and Mon

Le Potager du Roy (€–€€)
Good-value, well-kept place with a pleasantly old-fashioned air and traditional cooking.
✉ 1 rue du Maréchal-Joffre, 78000 Versailles ☎ 01 39 50 35 34 🕐 Lunch, dinner; closed Sun and Mon

VINCENNES
🚇 Porte de Vincennes

Ristoriante Alessandro (€–€€)
If the setting is plain enough at this pizzeria beside the town hall, the food is excellent Italian fare. Besides crispy, authentic pizzas, look out for seafood pastas and interesting *antipasti*. Good-value, weekday lunches and children's menus too.
✉ 51 rue de Fontenay, 94300 Vincennes ☎ 01 49 57 05 30 🕐 Lunch, dinner; closed Sun, 2 weeks in Aug

Paris

With so much to see in Paris, if you are making only a short visit, it is worth deciding in advance what you really want to see. For splendid city views, head for the Eiffel Tower, the Pompidou Centre or Montmartre's Sacré-Coeur. For art lovers, the Louvre, the Musée d'Orsay and the Musée Rodin stand out among a rich store of museums and galleries. For spectacular cathedrals, Notre-Dame and Sacré-Coeur are essential viewing.

For shopping, don't miss the area around Faubourg-St-Honoré and the Champs-Élysées. For a leisurely taste of traditional Paris, take a boat trip down the River Seine.

CENTRE GEORGES POMPIDOU

More than a mere landmark in the extensive face-lift that Paris has undergone since the 1970s, the high-tech Centre Georges Pompidou (known to Parisians as Beaubourg) is a hive of changing cultural activity. Contemporary art, architecture, design, photography, theatre, cinema and dance are all represented, while the lofty structure itself offers exceptional views over central Paris. Take the transparent escalator tubes for a bird's-eye view of the piazza where jugglers, artists, musicians and portrait artists strut their stuff in front of the teeming crowds.

www.centrepompidou.fr

✉ Place Georges Pompidou, 75004 ☎ 01 44 78 12 33 🕐 Wed–Mon 11–10. Museum and exhibits 11–9; Brancusi Workshop Wed–Mon 2–6; Library Mon, Wed–Fri noon–10, Sat–Sun 11–10 💷 Permanent collections inexpensive; full ticket expensive; free first Sun of every month 🍽 Restaurant (€€); café (€); snack bar (€) 🚇 Rambuteau, Hôtel de Ville, Châtelet 🚌 38, 47, 75 🚊 RER Line A, B, Châtelet-Les Halles ❓ Frequent lectures, concerts, parallel activities, Atelier des Enfants

CHAMPS-ÉLYSÉES/ARC DE TRIOMPHE

For most visitors this avenue epitomizes French elegance, but it is also a luxury shopping mall and a dazzling place of entertainment. The Champs-Élysées may be dominated by car showrooms, but plush cinemas, classy shops and one or two fashionable watering holes remain to tempt those who want to see and be seen. The Arc de Triomphe is an image of French national pride, built as a symbol of Napoleon's military strength. There is a wonderful view from the top, 50m (164ft) above street level.

✉ Champs-Élysées, 75008 🍴 Choice of restaurants (€–€€€) 🚇 Charles de Gaulle-Étoile, Georges V, Franklin D Roosevelt, Champs-Élysées-Clémenceau 🚌 31, 42, 73 ❓ Takes around 30 mins to walk from the Arc de Triomphe to place de la Concorde

JARDIN DU LUXEMBOURG

If you want to get away from the bustle during your trip to Paris these gardens are serene in all weathers and are the epitome of French landscaping. Attractions include shady chestnuts, potted orange and palm trees, lawns and even an experimental fruit garden and

orchard, while fountains, tennis courts, beehives, a puppet theatre and playgrounds offer other distractions. Joggers circle the gardens; sunbathers and bookworms settle into chairs. Statues of the queens of France, artists and writers are dotted about the gardens.

✉ Boulevard Saint-Michel, 75006 (various entries around the park) ☀ Daily dawn–dusk ✋ Free 🍴 Open-air cafés, kiosk restaurant (€–€€) Ⓜ Odéon 🚈 RER B Luxembourg
🚌 21, 27, 38, 82, 84, 85, 89

LOUVRE, MUSÉE DU

The world's largest museum was originally a medieval castle. It first took shape as an art gallery under François I, eager to display his Italian loot. The vast collection of some 30,000 exhibits is arranged on four floors of three wings, while beneath the elegant Cour Carrée (courtyard) lie the keep and dungeons of the original medieval fortress. Almost 5,000 years of art are covered, starting with Egyptian antiquities and culminating with European painting up to 1848.
www.louvre.fr

✉ 99 rue de Rivoli, 75001 ☎ 01 40 20 53 17 ☀ Wed–Mon 9–6, Wed and Fri 9am–10pm ✋ Moderate, inexpensive after 6pm Wed and Fri; free first Sun of every month 🍴 Restaurants and cafés (€–€€) Ⓜ Palais-Royal, Musée du Louvre
🚌 21, 24, 27, 39, 48, 68, 69, 72, 81, 95 ❓ Guided tours and audioguides

LE MARAIS

The sedate old-world atmosphere of this historic enclave at the heart of the city is unique, full of architectural beauty and cultural diversity. It offers visitors narrow picturesque streets, cafés and bistros, elegant mansions, tiny boutiques and a lively population. Across on the Left Bank you will find the Quartier Latin (Latin Quarter), a trendy student district.

✉ Le Marais 🚇 St-Paul, Rambuteau, Hôtel de Ville 🚌 29, 75, 96

MONTMARTRE/SACRÉ-COEUR

Once the haunt of famous artists, Montmartre retains something of a village atmosphere and the area has become a major tourist attraction. At the top of the village is the basilica of **Sacré-Coeur,** an unmistakable feature of the Paris skyline that magnetizes the crowds arriving either by funicular or via the steep steps of the terraced garden. The view of Paris is breathtaking, stretching for 50km (30 miles).

The dome is the second-highest point in Paris after the Eiffel Tower.

✉ Monmartre, 75018 🅰 Abbesses, Lamarck-Caulaincourt 🚌 Montmartrobus

Sacré-Coeur

www.sacre-coeur-montmartre.com

✉ Place du Parvis du Sacré-Coeur, 75018 ☎ 01 53 41 89 00 🕐 Basilica: daily 6am–10:30pm; dome and crypt: 9–5:30 (7 in summer) 🎫 Basilica and crypt: free; dome: inexpensive 🅰 Abbesses (from here, walk along rue Yvonne Le Tac, then take funicular or walk up steps) 🚌 30, 31, 54, 80, 85 Montmartrobus

NOTRE-DAME/RIVER SEINE

Notre Dame is a masterpiece of Gothic architecture and one of Paris's most famous landmarks with its 90m (295ft) spire and flying buttresses. You can admire it if you take a boat trip along the Seine. There are many splendid monuments to see along the river banks in particular on the Île Saint-Louis and the Île de la Cité, the historic centre of Paris.

Notre-Dame

www.cathedraledeparis.com

✉ Place du Parvis Notre-Dame 75004 ☎ 01 42 34 56 10; crypt 01 43 29 83 51 ⏰ Cathedral: daily 8–6:45 (7:45pm Sat–Sun). Tower and Treasury: daily 10–6:30, Apr–Sep (also until 11pm Sat–Sun, Jun–Aug); 10–5:30, rest of year.
✋ Cathedral: free; Tower and Treasury: moderate 🚇 Cité, St-Michel 🚌 21, 24, 27, 47
🚊 RER Lines B and C, St-Michel
❓ Free guided tours in English Wed, Thu, Sat 2pm

TOUR EIFFEL

Paris's most famous landmark has been towering above the city for more than a hundred years, yet its universal appeal remains constant. Built for the World Exhibition in 1889 by Gustave Eiffel, measuring 324m (1,063ft) in height, it was then the tallest building in the world and an unprecedented technological achievement. Its iron frame weighs 7,000 tonnes and 40 tonnes of paint are used to repaint it every seven years. There are three levels, all accessible by lift or stairs – a breathtaking 1,710 steps to the final stage. The genius of the construction shows in the fact that the tower sways no more than 9cm (3.5in) in high winds. It remained the world's highest structure for more than 40 years.

www.tour-eiffel.fr

✉ Champ de Mars, 75007 ☎ 01 44 11 23 23 🕐 Daily 9:30am–11pm (stairs 9:30–6:30; midnight in summer; last admission 30 mins before closing)

💶 First stage inexpensive; second stage moderate; final stage expensive; stairs inexpensive 🍴 Restaurants (€–€€€) Ⓜ Bir-Hakeim 🚌 42, 69, 72, 82, 87 🚆 RER Line C, Champs de Mars, Tour Eiffel

HOTELS

Hôtel de l'Abbaye (€€€)
A roaring log fire and a delightful inner garden ensure comfort whatever the season.

✉ 10 rue Cassette, 75006 ☎ 01 45 44 38 11; www.hotel-abbaye.com
🚇 St-Sulpice

Hôtel d'Angleterre (€€–€€€)
The largest rooms of this quiet luxury hotel overlook a lovely secluded garden.

✉ 44 rue Jacob, 75006 ☎ 01 42 60 34 72; www.hotel-dangleterre.com
🚇 St-Germain-des-Prés

Hôtel du Bois (€€)
Situated in a smart district 200m (220yds) from the Arc de Triomphe and Champs-Élysées, this hotel has small but elegant bedrooms decorated in warm soft tones.

✉ 11 rue du Dôme, 75016 ☎ 01 45 00 31 96; www.hoteldubois.com
🚇 Kléber, Charles de Gaulle-Étoile

Hôtel Esmeralda (€)
Some of the rooms in this old-fashioned yet cosy hotel offer delightful views of Notre-Dame. Very reasonably priced. No lift.

✉ 4 rue St-Julien-le-Pauvre, 75005 ☎ 01 43 54 19 20 🚇 St-Michel

Hôtel Franklin-Roosevelt (€€€)
Bright comfortable bedrooms with striking murals and functional bathrooms. You are assured of a warm welcome.

✉ 18 rue Clément Marot, 75008 ☎ 01 53 57 49 50; www.hroosevelt.com
🚇 Franklin D Roosevelt

Hôtel du Jeu de Paume (€€€)
Exclusive hotel on the Île Saint-Louis, housed in the converted Jeu de Paume (inside tennis court), with striking galleries and mezzanines. Beautiful marble bathrooms.

✉ 54 rue St-Louis-en-l'Île, 75004 ☎ 01 43 26 14 18;
www.hoteljeudepaume.com 🚇 Pont Marie

Hôtel Lenox (€€)

The Lenox, in the Saint-Germain district, is elegantly furnished and popular with the design and fashion set. Breakfast is served in a vaulted cellar.

✉ 9 rue de l'Université, 75007 ☎ 01 42 96 10 95; www.lenoxsaintgermain.com 🚇 St-Germain-des-Prés

Hôtel du Lys (€)

Simple hotel at the heart of the Quartier Latin; no lift but modern bathrooms, warm welcome and reasonable prices; book well in advance.

✉ 23 rue Serpente, 75006 ☎ 01 43 26 97 57; www.hoteldulys.com 🚇 St-Michel, Odéon

Hôtel de Nevers (€)

Simple but charming, in a former convent building; private roof terraces for top-floor rooms.

✉ 83 rue du Bac, 75007 ☎ 01 45 44 61 30 🚇 Rue du Bac

Hôtel du Panthéon (€€–€€€)

An elegant hotel conveniently situated in the university district, with well-appointed, air-conditioned bedrooms.

✉ 19 place du Panthéon, 75005 ☎ 01 43 54 32 95; www.hoteldupantheon.com 🚇 Cardinal-Lemoine

Hôtel La Perle (€€)

With 38 attractive rooms, this hotel in a renovated 17th-century building is in a quiet street near place St-Sulpice in the Saint-Germain-des-Prés district. Pretty flowered courtyard.

✉ 14 rue des Canettes, 75006 ☎ 01 43 29 10 10; www.hotellaperle.com 🚇 St-Germain-des-Prés

Hôtel de la Place des Vosges (€)

Picturesque quiet hotel in a 17th-century town house, just off the place des Vosges. Lovely views across the rooftops.

✉ 12 rue de Birague, 75004 ☎ 01 42 72 60 46; http://hotelplacedesvosges.com 🚇 St-Paul, Bastille

Hôtel Le Régent (€€–€€€)

Air-conditioning and bright, well-appointed bedrooms in this
cleverly restored 18th-century house in Saint-Germain-des-Prés.

✉ 61 rue Dauphine, 75006 ☎ 01 46 34 59 80; www.regent-paris-hotel.com
🚇 Odéon

Hôtel Relais Bosquet (€€)

Only a 10-minute walk from the Eiffel Tower and close to Les
Invalides, the hotel is spacious and comfortable. You can eat your
breakfast overlooking a pretty terrace.

✉ 19 rue du Champ-de-Mars, 75007 ☎ 01 47 05 25 45;
www.relaisbosquet.com 🚇 École-Militaire

Hôtel Relais du Louvre (€€)

Warm colours, antique furniture and modern comfort, a stone's
throw from the Louvre.

✉ 19 rue des Prêtres St-Germain-l'Auxerrois, 75001 ☎ 01 40 41 96 42;
www.relaisdulouvre.com 🚇 Louvre-Rivoli

Hôtel Ritz (€€€)

Sometimes called the palace of kings and the king of palaces.
Overlooking the place Vendôme, it boasts a beautiful swimming
pool and luxury fitness centre; prices are very high.

✉ 15 place Vendôme, 75001 ☎ 01 43 16 30 30; www.ritzparis.com
🚇 Opéra

Hôtel Saint-Honoré (€)

A one-star hotel on the chic rue St-Honoré on the Right Bank.
Pristine décor in the 29 rooms. Parking close by.

✉ 85 rue St-Honoré, 75001 ☎ 01 42 21 46 96; www.hotelsthonore.com
🚇 Châtelet

Hôtel Sunny (€)

A welcoming, renovated, two-star hotel with 37 rooms in the
Quartier Latin.

✉ 48 boulevard du Port Royal, 75005 ☎ 01 43 31 79 86;
www.hotelsunny.com 🚇 Les Gobelins

Timhôtel Jardin des Plantes (€)
Attractive, 33-roomed hotel in the Quartier Latin, opposite the botanical gardens and the Natural History Museum.

✉ 5 rue Linné, 75005 ☎ 01 47 07 06 20; www.timhotel.com 🚇 Jussieu

Timhôtel Montmartre (€€)
In the old part of Montmartre, halfway up the hill, with lovely views; attention to detail makes it a comfortable if simple place to stay.

✉ 11 rue Ravignan, 75018 ☎ 01 42 55 74 79; www.timhotel.com
🚇 Abbesses

RESTAURANTS

L'Alsace (€€)
Alsatian specialities and seafood; terrace in summer.

✉ 39 avenue des Champs-Élysées, 75008 ☎ 01 53 93 97 00 🕐 24 hours
🚇 Franklin D Roosevelt

Bistro Romain (€–€€)
One of 15 Bistro Romain restaurants in Paris. This one, in the Champs-Élysées, has an opulent setting. The food is basic pasta but there's plenty of it. Some dishes, including the chocolate mousse, are on an 'as much as you can eat' basis.

✉ 26 avenue des Champs-Élysées, 75008 ☎ 01 53 75 17 84 🕐 Daily 11:30am–1am 🚇 Franklin D Roosevelt

Blue Elephant (€€)
Thai cuisine in a fine setting near Bastille. Try the *chiang rai*.

✉ 43 rue de la Roquette, 75011 ☎ 01 47 00 42 00 🕐 Lunch, dinner; closed Sat lunch 🚇 Voltaire, Bastille

Boulangerie Paul (€)
Have a coffee, tea or hot chocolate at this attractively decorated bakery and try one of their delicious pastries. Also all sorts of specialized breads, from multi-grains to bacon bread.

✉ 77 rue de Seine, 75006 ☎ 01 55 42 02 23 🕐 Daily 7:30am–8pm
🚇 Odéon

Le Ciel de Paris (€€–€€€)

On the 56th floor of the Tour Montparnasse and said to be the highest restaurant in Europe. Enjoy the views while you eat.

✉ Tour Montparnasse, 33 avenue du Maine, 75015 ☎ 01 40 64 77 64
🕐 Lunch, dinner 🚇 Montparnasse-Bienvenüe

Coffee Parisien (€)

A Parisian bistro serving American diner-style food in Saint Germain-des-Prés. Good Sunday brunch and cheeseburgers.

✉ 4 rue Princesse, 75006 ☎ 01 43 54 18 18 🕐 Lunch, dinner 🚇 Mabillon, St-Germain-des-Prés

La Coupole (€€)

Famous brasserie from the 1920s with art deco setting and excellent seafood. Reasonable late-night menu (after 11pm).

✉ 102 boulevard du Montparnasse, 75014 ☎ 01 43 20 14 20 🕐 Daily 8:30am–1am 🚇 Vavin

El Fogón (€–€€)

Spanish cuisine in an attractive setting along the embankment between Notre-Dame and the Pont Neuf. Plentiful helpings of paella and *tapas*.

✉ 45 quai des Grands-Augustins, 75006 ☎ 01 43 54 49 73 🕐 Closed Sun
🚇 St-Michel

Fouquet's (€€)

Try this popular Parisian institution on the Champs-Élysées, an excellent spot for people-watching. A snack menu can be found in the bar or on the terrace.

✉ 99 avenue des Champs-Élysées, 75008 ☎ 01 40 69 60 50 🕐 Lunch, dinner 🚇 George V

Hard Rock Café (€–€€)

Relaxed atmosphere and plenty of buzz for eating hamburgers, fries, grills and steaks and enjoying milkshakes.

✉ 14 boulevard Montmartre, 75009 ☎ 01 53 24 60 00 🕐 Daily 9am–1am
🚇 Grands-Boulevards

Hippopotamus (€–€€)

With nearly 20 outlets of this chain in Paris you can be sure of a good grill and salad in a child-friendly environment. Good prices.

✉ 1 boulevard Beaumarchais, 75004 ☎ 01 44 61 90 40 🕔 Daily 11am–3am 🚇 Bastille

Le Procope (€–€€)

An 18th-century literary café known to Voltaire and Benjamin Franklin, and now an historic monument.

✉ 13 rue l'Ancienne Comédie, 75006 ☎ 01 40 46 79 00 🕔 Lunch, dinner 🚇 Odéon

La Rôtisserie d'En Face (€€)

Jacques Cagna's elegant brasserie across the street from his gastronomic restaurant, offering the likes of rabbit terrine and spit-roasted chicken.

✉ 2 rue Christine, 75006 ☎ 01 43 26 40 98 🕔 Closed Sat lunch, Sun 🚇 St-Michel

Senderens (€€€)

Haute cuisine in an authentic late 19th-century building with décor by Pajorelle. Try the roast duck with honey and spices or the delicious saddle of lamb.

✉ 9 place de la Madeleine, 75008 ☎ 01 42 65 22 90 🕔 Lunch, dinner 🚇 Madeleine

Terminus Nord (€€)

A 1920s-style brasserie near the Gard du Nord; the speciality is duck *foie gras* with apple and raisins. Also serves seafood.

✉ 23 rue de Dunkerque, 75010 ☎ 01 42 85 05 15 🕔 Lunch, dinner 🚇 Gare du Nord

Train Bleu (€€)

Brasserie with late 19th-century décor illustrating the journey from Paris to the Mediterranean.

✉ Place Louis Armand, Gare de Lyon, 75012 ☎ 01 43 43 09 06 🕔 Lunch, dinner 🚇 Gare de Lyon

SHOPPING

CHAMPS-ÉLYSÉES AND RUE DU FAUBOURG SAINT-HONORÉ

Most top fashion houses are situated in the Champs-Élysées area, in particular, avenue Montaigne, avenue Marigny and rue du Faubourg Saint-Honoré. The latter – take the métro to Concorde – is home to all the top names, including Prada (No 6), Hermès (No 24), Yves Saint Laurent (No 38) and Versace (No 62); you will also find top jewellers such as Cartier (No 17). Window-shopping is a great pastime if you can't afford the high prices.

For those on a tighter budget the Champs-Élysées is home to a number of high street chain stores and small shopping malls. Close by rue Royale and place de la Madeleine have some wonderful food shops, including the famous food hall, Fauchon.

Fauchon

✉ 26 place de la Madeleine, 75008 ☎ 01 70 39 38 00

🚇 Madeleine

BOULEVARD HAUSSMANN

Take the métro to Chaussée-d'Antin Lafayette and you'll emerge on boulevard Haussmann right opposite the stylish department store Galeries Lafayette. The store sells everything except menswear and food, which can be found in the building next door.

Down the street is the store's main competitor, Printemps – three buildings containing women's and children's fashion, homeware and menswear. You get a great view of Paris from the ninth floor of the Printemps de la Maison building. Chain stores such as Gap and H&M occupy the streets around the two stores.

Galeries Lafayette

✉ 40 boulevard Haussmann, 75009 ☎ 01 42 82 34 56 🚇 Chaussée d'Antin

Printemps

✉ 64 boulevard Haussmann, 75009 ☎ 01 42 82 50 00 🚇 Havre-Caumartin

LE MARAIS

This historic area with its narrow streets is home to some of Paris's best small one-off boutiques. This is a great place to wander and you will find plenty of restaurants when the shopping gets too tiring. As well as fashion items there are jewellery shops, home furnishings, designer office accessories, retro shops and second-hand clothes shops.

Take the métro to St Paul and have a look at the rue du Roi de Sicile for up-to-date clothing and accessories. Other interesting streets in Le Marais include rue des Francs-Bourgeois for fashion and rue Vieille-du-Temple, rue Debelleyme and rue St-Gilles for those who enthuse over art and antiques.

SAINT-GERMAIN-DES-PRÉS

Across the Seine by métro or on foot will bring you to the district of Saint-Germain-des-Prés on the Left Bank. The streets to the south and west of the métro station of Saint-Germain now house smarter designer shops, in addition to the more bohemian boutiques usually associated with this area.

In rue Bonaparte you will find names such as Louis Vuitton, Emporio Armani and Max Mara and in the rue St Sulpice more boutiques and smart shoe shops. In the rue de Sèvres is Paris's oldest department store – Bon Marché Rive Gauche – famous for its Grande Epicerie, selling specialities from various countries and freshly prepared delicacies, as well as designer clothes, household linens and haberdashery. In the rue de Grenelle are more shoe shops and designer labels, as well as shops with classy furniture and fragrant perfume.

Bon Marché Rive Gauche

✉ 24 rue de Sèvres, 75007 ☎ 01 44 39 80 00 🚇 Sèvres-Babylone

CARRÉ 'RIVE GAUCHE'

The 'square' formed along the Left Bank by the quai Voltaire, rue de l'Université, rue du Bac and rue des Saints-Pères, which also incorporates the rue de Verneuil, rue de Lille and rue de Beaune, is famous for its concentration of antiques dealers.

Index

Acknowledgements

The Automobile Association would like to thank the following photographers, companies and picture libraries in the preparation of this book.

Abbreviations for the picture credits are as follows – (t) top; (b) bottom; (l) left; (r) right; (c) center; (AA) AA World Travel Library.

4l Sleeping Beauty's Castle, ©Disney; 4c Disneyland Park entrance in Winter, ©Disney ; 4r Sleeping Beauty Castle, ©Disney; 5l Cabane de Robinson, ©Disney; 5c Vaux-le-Vicomte, AA/B Rieger; 5r Vaux-le-Vicomte, AA/B Rieger; 6/7 Sleeping Beauty's Castle, ©Disney; 8/9 Fantasyland in Summer, ©Disney; 10bl Lilly's Boutique, ©Disney; 10br Catastrophe Canyon, ©Disney; 10/11 "Rendezvous with the Stars" Restaurant, ©Disney; 11t Frontierland Gardens in Spring, ©Disney; 11r Fantasia Gardens in Springtime, ©Disney; 12l Rainforest Café, ©Disney; 12/13t California Grill Restaurant, ©Disney; 12/13b Production Courtyard, ©Disney; 14 Silver Spur Steakhouse, ©Disney; 15t Backlot Express Restaurant, ©Disney; 15c Plaza Gardens Restaurant, ©Disney; 16/17 Space Mountain, Mission 2, ©Disney; 18/19 Lucky Nugget Saloon, ©Disney; 20/21 Disneyland Park entrance in Winter, ©Disney; 24/25 Disneyland Resort Paris at night, ©Disney; 27 Disneyland Park, ©Disney; 29 Gare du Nord station, AA/C Sawyer; 30/31 Paris Metro Station, AA/C Sawyer; 32 Paris Phonebox, AA/K Paterson; 36/37 Sleeping Beauty Castle, ©Disney; 40/41 Disneyland Park entrance, ©Disney; 42/43 Little Girl with Mickey Mouse balloon, ©Disney; 46 Bust of Walt Disney, ©Disney; 49 Main Street Shop, ©Disney; 50 Adventureland, ©Disney; 52 Prince Ali, ©Disney; 53 Big Thunder Mountain by night, ©Disney; 54 Meet and Greet, ©Disney; 57 Fastpass logo, ©Disney; 60/61 Disney Village by Night, ©Disney; 64/65 "Tinkerbell's Fantasy in the Sky" Fireworks, ©Disney; 68 A Magical day at Disneyland Pars, ©Disney; 71 Sleeping Boy, ©Disney; 72/73 Cabane de Robinson, ©Disney; 74 Disneyland Park entrance, ©Disney; 75 Disneyland Park logo, ©Disney; 76t Main Street logo, ©Disney; 76b Main Street USA, décor, ©Disney; 77 City Hall, ©Disney; 78t Liberty Arcade, ©Disney; 78b Main Street USA, ©Disney; 80/81 Wonderful World of Disney Parade, ©Disney; 82/83 Wonderful World of Disney Parade, ©Disney; 83 Main Street vehicles, ©Disney; 84 Fuente del Oro Restaurant, ©Disney; 85 Frontierland logo, ©Disney; 86/87 Big Thunder Mountain, ©Disney; 88 Cottonwood Creek Ranch, ©Disney; 88/89 Chip 'n' Dale in Frontierland, ©Disney; 90 Phantom Manor, ©Disney; 91t Phantom Manor, ©Disney; 91b Phantom Manor, ©Disney; 92/93 Rustler Roundup Shootin Gallery, ©Disney; 93 Frontierland, ©Disney; 94 Adventureland logo, ©Disney; 95 Adventureland Bazaar Entrance, ©Disney; 96/97 Captain Hook's Galley, ©Disney; 97 Indiana Jones and the Temple of Peril, ©Disney; 98 Pirates of the Caribbean, ©Disney; 98/99 Pirates of the Caribbean, ©Disney; 99 La Cabane de Robinson, ©Disney; 100 Fantasyland logo, ©Disney; 100/101 The Enchanted Fairytale Ceremony, ©Disney; 102 Alice's Curious Labyrinth, ©Disney; 103 Kids go Free – Dumbo, ©Disney; 104 It's a Small World, ©Disney; 104/105 Mad Hatter's Tea Cups, ©Disney; 106t Sleeping Beauty's Castle, ©Disney; 106b Sleeping Beauty's Castle, ©Disney; 107 Snow White and the Seven Dwarves, ©Disney; 108t Discoveryland logo, ©Disney; 108/109 Space Mountain, Mission 2, ©Disney; 109 Autopia, ©Disney; 110/111 Orbitron, machines, ©Disney; 112 Space Mountain, ©Disney; 113 Star Tours, ©Disney; 114 The Legend of the Lion King Show, ©Disney; 114/115 The Legend of the Lion King Show, ©Disney; 116/117 Studio 1 entrance, ©Disney; 117 Walt Disney Studios logo, ©Disney; 118t Front Lot logo, ©Disney; 118c Disney Studio 1 detail, ©Disney; 119 Walt Disney Studio Stores Boutique, ©Disney; 120t BackLot logo, ©Disney; 120b Television production tour, ©Disney; 121 Moteurs Action! Stunt show spectacular, ©Disney; 122/123 Flying Carpets over Agrabah, ©Disney; 122 Art of Disney Animation, ©Disney; 124 Production Courtyard logo, ©Disney; 124/125 Cyberspace Attraction, ©Disney; 154/155 Vaux-le-Vicomte, AA/B Rieger; 157 Fontainebleau, AA/D Noble; 159 Vaux-le-Vicomte, AA/B Rieger; 160/161 Versailles gardens, AA/M Jourdan; 162 Vicennes, AA/J A Tims; 163 Sealife Paris sign, ©Disney; 168/169 Montmartre, AA/P Enticknap; 171t Centre Georges Pompidou, AA/J A Tims; 171b Centre Georges Pompidou, AA/C Sawyer; 172 Arc de Triomphe, AA/K Paterson; 172/173 Louvre, AA/M Jourdan; 173 Jardin du Luxembourg, AA/M Jourdan; 174t Le Marais, AA/M Jourdan; 174b Montmartre, AA/P Enticknap; 175 Sacre Coeur, AA/A Souter; 176 Notre Dame, AA/C Sawyer; 176/177 Notre Dame, AA/A Souter; 177/178 Eiffel Tower, AA/B Rieger

Every effort has been made to trace the copyright holders, and we apologise in advance for any unintentional omissions or errors. We would be pleased to apply any corrections in any following edition of this publication.

Dear Reader

Your comments, opinions and recommendations are very important to us. Please help us to improve our travel guides by taking a few minutes to complete this simple questionnaire.

You do not need a stamp (unless posted outside the UK). If you do not want to cut this page from your guide, then photocopy it or write your answers on a plain sheet of paper.

Send to: **The Editor, AA World Travel Guides,**
FREEPOST SCE 4598, Basingstoke RG21 4GY.

Your recommendations...

We always encourage readers' recommendations for restaurants, nightlife or shopping – if your recommendation is used in the next edition of the guide, we will send you a **FREE AA Guide** of your choice from this series. Please state below the establishment name, location and your reasons for recommending it.

_____
_____
_____
_____
_____
_____

Please send me **AA Guide** _____

About this guide...

Which title did you buy?

   AA _____

Where did you buy it?_____

When? m m / y y

Why did you choose this guide? _____
_____
_____
_____
_____

Did this guide meet your expectations?

Exceeded ☐   Met all ☐   Met most ☐   Fell below ☐

Were there any aspects of this guide that you particularly liked? _____
_____
_____
_____

continued on next page...

Is there anything we could have done better? _____

_____

_____

_____

About you...

Name (*Mr/Mrs/Ms*) _____

Address _____

_____

_____ Postcode

Daytime tel nos _____

Email _____

Please only give us your mobile phone number or email if you wish to hear from us about other products and services from the AA and partners by text or mms, or email.

Which age group are you in?
Under 25 ☐ 25–34 ☐ 35–44 ☐ 45–54 ☐ 55–64 ☐ 65+ ☐

How many trips do you make a year?
Less than one ☐ One ☐ Two ☐ Three or more ☐

Are you an AA member? Yes ☐ No ☐

About your trip...

When did you book? m m / y y   When did you travel? m m / y y

How long did you stay? _____

Was it for business or leisure? _____

Did you buy any other travel guides for your trip?

If yes, which ones? _____

_____

_____

Thank you for taking the time to complete this questionnaire. Please send it to us as soon as possible, and remember, you do not need a stamp (*unless posted outside the UK*).

AA Travel Insurance call **0800 072 4168** or visit www.theAA.com